The
Total Joy
of Travelling on
Public Transport

Phil Lowe

ISBN: 978-0-244-23551-2

PublishNation
www.publishnation.co.uk

Author's Preface

Ah, the total *joy* of travelling on public transport. Do you love travelling with the delightfully varied public and their dubious electronic gadgets and often odious habits? Do you mind when the person behind you has a full blown argument on their mobile phone with the speaker positioned at extra loud, just so you are sure to get both argumentative sides of the mutual yelling? Is it OK for someone to apply their nail polish on a hot bus, thereby nearly choking the other passengers to death with the toxic fumes? Would special mobile confessionals built into modes of public transport ease the congestion of verbal diarrhoea from total strangers? Do you balk at getting up close and personal with the great unwashed? Are you the kind of person that finds the joys of travelling on public transport highly amusing or, would you rather just throw yourself under a bus?

Many thousands of people in Great Britain travel to work and back on public transport. We commuters use the buses, trains and trams, on average, around five days of the week. We endure the pleasure of other passengers talking loudly on their mobiles. Season after season, we delight in strangers coughing their germ clustered spittle all over us, almost to the point where we wonder if it is actually raining inside the vehicle. Some other passengers sit crunching sweets like a starving deaf horse and some salivate wildly as they delve into endless bags of stinky squid and blue cheese flavoured crisps. And, quite often – well, let's just say it - it gets much worse! I know. I have been there. I mislaid the tee shirt and bought an annual travel pass.

I used to work for a major supermarket as a butcher and fishmonger. During my eight and a half years of working there I made twenty combined bus and tram journeys a week to work. That's four a day, five days a week, totalling approximately a thousand minutes or sixteen and a half hours sitting on public transport in order to get to work. That's proper commitment for you. Most days the commuting necessitated early morning travel and late afternoon returning home in the rush hour traffic. On a Thursday and Friday it was midday travel to work and then I'd be travelling home at night with a bus load of excitable half naked and semi pissed young folk heading into Nottingham to go clubbing. Or whatever young folk do these days. Half naked and pissed Bible study perhaps.

Occasionally I read whilst travelling, but mostly I just people watched. It was fascinating. As a writer and observer of life I was making notes and sometimes recording my observations onto a Dictaphone and trying not to be obvious about it. My inner comedian regularly found himself seeking out comedy gold in the habits and relationships of my fellow travellers. When the chance came, I would write my wry observations down in a notebook or on scraps of paper at work. Little did I realise how useful they would be as *aide memoires* in eventually writing this book.

It was just a writer's habit to document things and to amuse myself at the time. Like many people, I love to people watch but less (first joke alert) through high powered binoculars these days. Often events were funny or disturbing or even both and I assumed I would definitely remember them without recording them in some way. Even an hour later I would be trying to tell a quirky travelling incident to a mate at work and I would struggle to recall what had made me smile or nearly throw up on the journey. Try doing those both at once. Or better still, don't. Eventually, once this book seemed like it was going to be a reality, I made it a rule to make sure I documented.

Most of the stories in this book are focussed on my travels around Nottinghamshire. Some of the stories occurred at the time when the Broadmarsh shopping centre bus station existed. It has since been demolished and now the massive building site is slowly being re-developed into a new travel centre with a new bus station. No doubt, the poorly looking black foot pigeons that made their crude razor wire edged homes, in and around the old bus station, will return to re-home themselves in the future pigeon friendly, steel and glass palace of bus travel. In the meantime they will be putting their crippled avian feet up in sunny Spain and knocking back the Spanish beers whilst topping up their suntans. Who can blame them? Sometimes, I wish I was a pigeon.

Critically, a few years ago, a new tram line was built and I made full use of it to convey me from Nottingham to work in the small town of Beeston. I was delighted by this as it often meant less bus travel where it felt it was like travelling in a mobile doctor's surgery where all the travellers violently coughed and sneezed throughout the journey. Or as I half jokingly called it – the voyage of the eternally damned.

Life can be as random as getting on the wrong bus twice in one day and believe me I have done that. Reflecting that, the nature of this book wryly meditates on my travelling life in the following non-chronological and I suppose, rather random stories, of the total *joys* of a daily bus and tram commute to work. So, lovely readers, please dip into my amusing retrospective tales and enjoy my surreal humour. Like most forays into the public arena of life one encounters a degree of bad language and references to sex. Shock horror! This book has its share of these but my main reason for writing this is to share my experiences and daft flights of fancy. Enjoy the ride and hold on tight! Ding ding!

Phil Lowe

Anonymous quote about travel companions:
"It doesn't matter where you are going, it's who
you have beside you."

'I am sitting on the top deck of the number ten bus back to my village. It is rammed with passengers as it always is around four-thirty in the evening. One young woman sitting at the front is in conversation on her mobile. She is loud and garrulous and so far has been rabbiting on and on non-stop for twenty-five minutes. She hasn't yet taken a breath. Most of her sentences start with "Sooooo..." and she must be religious because she keeps saying "Oh My God!" As we get close to my stop she says in a rather dramatic tone "Oh My God! Seriously? Oh MY DAYS!!! I am literally speechless!" The whole top deck of commuters who have tolerated her insistent drivel burst out laughing at the irony! She has no sense of satire and carries on talking and talking and talking.'

Overheard comment: Woman helping another old lady set up a new mobile phone. "You need to look at your time zones Betty. You want United Kingdom. No love, not that one. You're not in Vietnam are you?"

'It is still dark this morning and the interior strip lights of the bus into town reflect in the front window of the bus. They look like ghostly antennae stretching out into the darkness. It is like the vehicle is morphing into a giant ant on wheels. Outside the street lights glow bright orange and the tinny rattle and whir of the momentum of the bus travelling at an average of forty miles an hour sounds, to the half awake me, like someone is tapping wire coat hangers on the roof of the bus. Perhaps I have drunk too much coffee already.'

Overheard comment: "It were full of them there cat fleas! I've been bitten all over!"

'On the tram now. It's six thirty-three in the morning so not many other people are travelling today. There's a bloke ahead who looks like he has been out on the town and trying to sleep it off. Someone has drawn the word 'twat' on his forehead in red lipstick. I bet he has no idea where he is going. The tram tannoy has just announced a stop. The sleeping drunk shouts "Who said that?!!" then immediately slumps back into his drunken stupor.'

'Today, not an enormous amount is happening on the route from my village to the main bus station in Nottingham. It is when I get the connecting bus from the Broadmarsh bus station to Beeston that things often become interesting. At the bus station itself I regularly see slumped individuals attempting to sleep sitting up on the cold, light green, metal benches and I wonder if they have actually been there all night and why. Some look lost and desperately trying to get a rest. Some look like they have spent the night on the town and are feeling queasy and very hung over as they wait numbly for a bus home. Others are surrounded by personal belongings and travel bags and a black lady I saw at seven am yesterday was sitting encircled and hemmed in by over thirty items of luggage. The missing twenty-nine owners of this mass of pink and purple luggage were still nowhere to be seen as my bus left the station.'

'There are very few people on this bus except four very common schoolgirls at the back. On a quick glance they all have their feet up on the seats and their skirts up around their bottoms. Best not to look as they seem like - not so bright girls - (I'm just too kind in my descriptions) who would enjoy confrontation. God's teeth, they are loud and they swear like fishwives. They seem to be enjoying their common notoriety and gobby bravado. One is on her mobile talking to some young man, one assumes. "Noooo! Fuck off. Fuck the fuck off!" she shrieks. More protesting issues forth. "Noooo. Tell him I don't give head!" Jesus H Christ! She must be all of twelve years old. After-note: Never have I been so pleased to get off a bus.'

'On a Sunday morning I occasionally witness some of the dodgier elements of society doing their edgy street-wise lope through the virtually empty Broadmarsh bus station. Most are hooded, proud of their gold teeth, gaunt individuals accompanied either by their trophy dogs, tattooed trophy girlfriends or slopping a can of Stella over themselves *en route* to the 24hour Booze Is Us store. I often score some class A drugs off them, pat their cute doggy whilst commenting on the similarity of the bling they are all sporting. That includes the dog. They have kindly invited me round to their gaff for high tea and muffins (laced with crack cocaine) at my own convenience. No doubt they will get out their best set of china.

I feel we could all be good friends if we tried. And there the fiction ends.'

'On weekday evenings the bus station is busy with commuters intending to travel by bus and, from time to time, I witness near death experiences of the travellers who race between the platforms in an attempt to get the 'just leaving' National Express to Luton, London or Brighton. As they frantically wave their arms and shout their frustrations at the departing bus they also neglect to see another speedily departing bus that violently hisses as it suddenly slams on its brakes to avoid crushing them.

Thankfully, I've yet to see a collision of human and speeding metal. Thankfully. The funniest version of this is when a whole family, often with all their mobile mass of suitcases and luggage in tow, race and weave their frantic way through the station and then miss the coach. They all pile to a sudden mortified halt as they watch the rear lights of the coach disappear into the busy outgoing traffic. Once they have caught their collective breath one of their party will get loudly bollocked for making them late. It's usually a man.'

'I sometimes wish I drove a car so as to be in a position where I didn't have to listen to all the crap people gabble on about on public transport. One gets a percentage of people, men and women, who seemingly have no perception that they can be heard on their mobile phones droning continually, on and on, about nothing of actual worth. I've heard quite intimate arguments going off with the speaker noisily remonstrating with the listener about the sexual and social failures of their relationship. So much so, that the entire bus load of travellers should (in an ideal world) stand up *en mass* and tell the odious speaker to "Shut the f**k up!" Honesty!'

'This morning there was the man who, on a quiet Sunday morning journey, got on my bus and no sooner had he sat down than he was on his mobile and chit chatting to all of his lovely mates. His 'hot off the press' topics were about his night out on the town, his binge drinking antics, his sexual conquests, the fights he got involved in and football. I kid you not when I say that every second word was a variation on the expletive – fuck. This diatribe of fuck this, fucking that, the fucker who fucked up the game etcetera, was appalling. It was as if he couldn't speak without swearing and this went on for a good fifteen minutes until, exhausted, I got off the bus. When he wasn't saying the F word he interlaced his chats with other niceties such as "couldn't be arsed" and "it was shit." As I was getting off the bus I caught a glimpse of this rough, potato faced, verbally challenged thug re-arranging his dangly bits with an exploratory hand groping down his stained baggy trousers. How utterly charming for us all. Truly, it was akin to being in the presence of royalty without the corgis.'

'Once upon a short bus journey, there was a terribly thin old man with long silvery hair, dressed in a tatty overcoat and a phenomenally furry Russian hat. He stood all through my bus journey and stared vacantly ahead of himself. There were plenty of vacant seats, he just chose to stand. At one point in the journey he moved to some other seats and stood behind those with his scrawny hands holding tight around the top of the seat next to the back of some poor woman's head.'

'Recently, a scruffy late middle-aged man in a shiny track suit and blue woolly hat got on near the Old Market Place in the city. He had long grey/black greasy hair, the gritty repose of the constantly agitated, deep facial wrinkles and stunk of cigarette smoke as he abruptly pulled open the rectangular window above my seat and went storming off to the back of the bus. A few minutes later I thought that I heard the sound of an escaped snake some short distance behind me. Escaped snakes are a common occurrence on Nottingham's buses. I was about to ring the RSPCA when I realised that this bloke was liberally spraying himself with Lynx. The sickly sweet odour of men's deodorant drifted down the bus. I think he must have used the whole can given the density of the smell. If I was a fly I would have been spinning my last gasping death throws on the bus gangway.'

'Obviously it isn't all men that travel on buses and the other night, as I took my journey home by the University of Nottingham and the professional tennis centre, a group of young tennis players got on the bus. This group included three strapping lads loaded down with large sports bags and two rather attractive young blonde women wearing tennis attire. The girls in the tiny white tennis skirts were possibly Ukrainian and their startlingly white knickers possibly from Next. Myself and a few shy and retiring fellows sat facing them regularly got flashed at all the way back to Nottingham.'

'One small Nottinghamshire town called Beeston has a large Chinese, Japanese and Malaysian population. This is to do with the Nottingham University up the road having long term connections with these countries. Often, for the short ten minute bus ride between the Chinese supermarket on Beeston High Street and the Dunkirk area, west of the University, the bus fills up with polite Asian travellers and their many orange Sainsbury plastic carrier bags of food. They always brighten up my journey as they seem to be very happy and are always laughing amongst themselves. I like them so much I feel almost obliged to give them all a friendly wave as they gather together their, full to bursting bags, get off the bus and head off in the opposite direction, giggling.'

'I haven't seen this woman lately, but I used to encounter a very characterful lady bus driver. She was pleasantry personified or just plain crackers. When she wasn't coughing her – fifty fags a day – graveyard cough whilst driving the bus in the most original jerky fashion, she addressed all her passengers joining or leaving the bus as angel, sweetheart or darling. "Where are you going angel?" A return sweetheart?" "How're you then darling?" Everyone on the bus smiled at her dialogue but held on tightly to their seats as she, if you'll pardon the expression, jerked off down the high street.'

'A brief note for this morning because I am not sure I want to go too explicit in describing this actions of this man. There's a totally gross fellow male traveller seated not far behind me. He's making those constant wet snorting snot noises to the point where I am starting to feel sick. I may need to get off this bus and pick up the next one. I'll be late for work I know, but I don't care. I'm mentally willing him to ring the bell and get off before I do. He doesn't.'

'I'm tired now. It's been busy at work. Dogs. Great. There are two dogs on the bus without leashes. They're play fighting mid-aisle and the scruffy owner's just laughing at them. There is a real feeling of tension and I dare not move for fear of my legs being savaged.'

'A weird young couple are sitting in front of me on this Christmas Eve journey into Nottingham. Like the dogs in the previous story, they are play fighting, bickering, practically wrestling and fondling each other inappropriately. Not that the dogs fondled each other inappropriately. That would be beyond wrong. Back to the couple. He is behaving like a baby and a bully almost simultaneously and she is letting him. Jesus Christ! They are really getting on my wick. Why can't people just behave normally? Merry Christmas all.'

'Most mornings a late middle-aged lady gets on the bus in Nottingham and hums a sad and thankless ditty with four repeats on the same theme whilst sat behind me. It turns out she is knitting what looks like a very long blue scarf. I call her Lady Knits The Blues. I now have a very tiresome ear worm based on her four note tune.'

'A man in a green top has just coughed violently. He has sent an arc of fine spittle over the heads of any passengers unlucky enough to sit in the front of him. He must have missed the lessons on holding one's hand in front of the coughing mouth. Or maybe he just doesn't give a toss. There are now several people unsure whether to wipe the wetness off themselves with their bare hand or just leave it. Gross.'

'My journey's peace is often broken by the person who feels the need to 'snap' their newspaper instead of gently turning the pages. Remember those 'snappers' we used to get free in comics in the 1960s? They were triangular shaped paper toys that made a surprisingly loud crack when the holder percussed the object away from them. Today's snappy experience with the newspaper is like that, but sadly without the benefits of Dennis the Menace, the Bash Street Kids and Korky the Kat.'

Overheard comment: "I like to use a plastic bag and a rolling pin and just bash the hell out of it."

'Of course there are always the loud mobile phone users on public transport. I speak in particular of this cleaning lady I'm overhearing right now. She works at Nottingham University. She is called Dotty or Dorothy, dependent to whom she is talking. How do I know this? She phones her family and feels the need to bellow down the phone. Her unfortunate family must all be deaf because Dotty has to tell them several times that it is, indeed she, and each exclamation gets louder and louder. One time she bellows so loud that all the autumn leaves at the side of the bus shoot up Wizard of Oz tornado style, turning the landscape into a blur of brown, red and gold. A passing cyclist loses his cloth cap in the tremendous gust. The bus destination panel changes instantly to Kansas. Tapping together my sparkly red shoes makes no difference whatsoever to the situation. Sometimes, when travelling, 'There's no place like home - Toto.'

'There's a decidedly inebriated and skinny man down the bus fluctuating between being asleep and cursing. The self-same prune faced guy has woken up and has begun alternating between swigging the remains of his sherry and singing Rod Stewart's song Maggie May whilst also hinting that he's going to throw up. Worried that he might, I got off this bus and away from the drunk at the Queens Medical Centre. I joined another bus five minutes later. The new driver told me and the other passengers not to venture towards the back of the bus as someone had had a sick 'accident'. Lord above! After that God forsaken journey I needed a stiff drink!'

'I wonder if these old ladies would be offended if I wrote out and passed them a note saying, 'Thanks for sitting next to me but, dearest of old ladies, I do not need to have my nostrils assailed by the acidic aroma of decades worth of old urine. Nor do I need to hear your laborious stories of yesteryear and your intense family dramas complete with arm waving actions and your frequent need to fondle my left knee. Lastly, I am too old to be your toy boy.'

'I encounter drunk young men and women on a regular basis in and around Nottingham. The city is no different to most British cities on a Friday and Saturday night in this 'cultural' regard. When I took my tired feet to the main bus station, one evening after work, an older couple were actually having a running physical and verbal battle. The gentle dialogue went "You fecker!" this and "You feckin' fecker! I'll feckin' have you!"that. My thoughts, as I sat on my bus, that was about to leave the station in five minutes, were "Please don't get on my bus. Please." To sweet natured me it was incredulous that they were yelling abuse at each other in a public space. Shameless. Thankfully, they didn't get on my bus but only because one of them was trying to uproot a full waste bin to launch at their beloved.'

Overheard comment: "There were feathers all over the front room and sparrow blood in places you wouldn't believe. Bloody cat."

'I spy a man in his mid-forties dressed in a sharp suit and Liam Gallagher style haircut with sideburns that went out of fashion at least a decade ago, as did Liam Gallagher. The man has been on his phone for quite a while now. I think he must be talking to someone at his office – very loudly. Don't they always? Myself and all the other passengers have heard all the private financial details of some housing deal including the names of the buyers and an account number. More details are spilling out of his mouth. He's just finished (we can only hope) and the last words he said were "Of course, that's just between us two." Does he think all the other people on the bus around him are deaf?'

'This story isn't just for today, but most days when I have been working on the fish counter. Although I wash my hands and take off my apron, overalls and ill fitting, feet destroying work boots, when I go home on the bus or tram, nobody wants to sit next to me. Do I smell vaguely of fish? I don't think so but other passengers are virtually hanging off the side of the public transport rather than sit next to me. Perhaps it has nothing to do with my paranoia about whiffing of sea bass and octopus and more to do with the public need to have a seat of their own and spread themselves out so nobody can sit next to them. Getting a phantom whiff of trout now. It's me isn't it?'

'The kids are back in town! Well, more precisely they are on the tram without paying. It's a game they can't play on the bus where you have to pay the driver or show a travel pass. How do I know they haven't paid? For a start they keep giggling, which is nothing unusual for a teenager. Then they get very attentive on their surroundings each time the tram approaches the next stop. Three of the gang are stationed along the length of the tram; one at each end and one in the middle. They know the inspectors' uniforms by sight and they crane their teenage necks to look out for them waiting on the tram stop platforms. If they spot the inspectors, who tend to approach from each end of the tram like a pincer movement, the kids all gather in the middle and stroll off with a group air of nonchalance and a barely disguised undercurrent of smirking and 'we got away with it again' giggles. Just don't get me started about when they swing like monkeys from the hand straps on the tram.'

'The bus was busy tonight and I put my big plastic carrier bag full of shopping down by my feet, out of the way. It was safe until another jumbo sized male passenger got on the bus and lumped himself next to me. This had the effect of virtually crushing me against the window for the half hour, stale body odour, filled journey. Somehow the man managed to land his size fifteen distinctly grubby trainers directly in the centre of my shopping bag. My chicken now has a zigzag pattern over the chicken breasts. Did he apologise? Of course not.'

Overheard comment: "It makes no sense to me. Not at my age. All of them hush tags on Facebook, whatever they are."

'There was another bickering couple on the bus today. From the smell of them I would say that booze fuelled their argument. Well, I say argument, more a one sided succession of savage snipes really. The man being abused just kept looking out of the window and onto the blurry world passing by. I guess he was wishing that she would just go away – forever. Like in an instant big puff of smoke. His unspoken sentiments were shared by all of the passengers and the bus driver on this journey. Her diatribe, where she put emphasis on certain words, went something like this; "YOU are winding me up! You listening? I said you ARE winding me up. Not only that but you are WINDING me up! Yeah? WINDING ME UP! You're not listening are you? Winding ME UP. You are winding me UP! And... I'm sick of it. You are a knob. A wind up knob and what's more all this bus knows you are a big useless knob." I'm sure she stole that speech from Shakespeare's As You Like It.'

'Too much information is often given on public transport. Not about the destinations or stops but, by the passengers themselves. A man just sat next to me. A complete stranger. His hair was greasy grey and his body odour a bit ripe especially on this warm summer's day. He said "I've just got out of the shower. The muck that streams off you sometimes is unbelievable, especially round your balls. Do you know what I mean?" Staring vacantly out of the window is my latest hobby.'

'There's a young boy on this bus journey saying 'hello' to everything that passes. It's quite cute. However, endearing innocence can wear very thin when the bus encounters a traffic jam. Here is a brief version of his endless high pitched 'hellos'. "Hello tree! Hello bird. Hello man. Hello baby. Hello house. Hello school. Hello pregnant lady. Oops! Hello cross fat lady. Hello ambulance. Hello police mister. Hello bus stop. Hello bell. Hello tickets. Hello hedges. Hello poplar. Hello birch. Hello oak. Hello children's book of trees. Hello sky! Hello clouds. Hello cumulus nimbus clouds. Hello red bike. Bye bye fat pregnant lady! Hello buggy. Hello traffic. Hello red light. Hello traffic. Hello red light. Hello more traffic. Hello red light. Hello red-faced man. Hello red light. Mummy why aren't we moving? Hello red light. Hello traffic. Hello orange light. Hello green light..." You get the picture now, I'm sure. Hello picture.'

'A bus is neither a crèche nor is it a brightly coloured kindergarten on wheels. Yes the wheels on the bus do go round and round but we don't need to hear a jaunty song about the fact for half a bloody hour. I know I sound like a right grumpy old sod but feeling forced to listen to young parents singing along with their three year old about Five Little Monkeys or I Want A Hippopotamus For Christmas or that damned bus song and its ever circulating wheels, is a pain in the ears. I didn't even know the songs before. but believe you me, boys and girls, I do now. My friendly ear worms have ensured that they have been trapped in my brain all day, and like the big friendly bus wheels, they go round and frigging round.'

Overheard comment: "If I wanted Twitter I'd get a budgie. Tweet it? Twat it more like."

'Hitler himself is sitting four seats down. I can't actually see his face now but I did when I passed him on the way to an empty tram seat. He still has the size twelve paintbrush moustache and the deeply etched lines of cruelty around his drooping mouth. I am surprised that nobody else on the tram has recognised him. The sweeping curtain hairstyle has got a bit out of control in his latter years and today he is wearing a yellow high vis jacket without swastika armband. Now he is getting off and gently ambling towards his discrete council estate bungalow hideaway named after the country, Argentina. In my imagination the bungalow features a concrete underground bunker and no expense spared, recreational, hot tub amenity. Even evil dictators have to relax somehow.'

'Fellow bus passenger Ashley, is a lucky chap. His friend has just pointed out several local benefits that will bring total bliss into Ashley's life. He doesn't need to win the National Lottery because all that he could ever want is right here in the Nottinghamshire town of Beeston. "Look Ashley." says the friend "You've got the chippy, you've got a Tesco Extra over there, you've got the bookies, you've got Wetherspoons, you've got online porn and you've got your benefits ant ya? (ant ya translates as - hasn't one?)" Lucky Ashley.'

'No trams on all routes this morning because of a police incident near Nottingham Trent University. It was later revealed there was a man on the loose with no tram ticket and armed with a machete. Police and tram authorities warned passengers that it is dangerous to travel on the tram without a ticket.'

'Before the new NET tram line from Clifton to Toton opened, I used to travel from work in Beeston to Nottingham city centre on the Trent Barton Indigo bus service. This meant using the bus late on a Friday night. The bus goes past the University and picks up the students for their fun night out in Nottingham. I had a connecting bus in Nottingham to take me to my village and it went just once an hour. Missing that would mean hanging around the bus station on a Friday night for a wasted hour when I would prefer to be home. I would get really annoyed at the queues of students getting on my first bus and fannying around as they got together the right change for the journey. Gone were the days when students would write a cheque out for the journey. Using actual coinage proved even more difficult somehow. This would mean unnecessary delays and sometimes the frustration of being on the Indigo bus literally watching my connecting bus sail off into the distance at night. I don't miss that.'

'Today turned out to be very dramatic at Nottingham Train Station. There was a fire in the ladies toilet on the concourse.

Six fire engines have been summoned to the fire and the whole railway station has been evacuated. It is a major incident and the railway station and tram stop above have been indefinitely closed to the public. Looks like I will be getting the bus to work for a few days now. I hope no-one was hurt.'

'This evening is the first evening of travelling by bus due to the fire incident at the railway station. The whole area is cordoned off. Peering into the now pitch black concourse as I pass on the bus is frightening. Although the firemen have put out the fire which spread upwards into the roof, there is still a strong smell of burning and acrid smoke in the air.'

'The railway station is now open again after about four days closure yet the Costa Coffee outlet and similar ones on the concourse, remain closed due to smoke damage. There is still a smoky haze in the air and a burnt wood and plastic smell remains from the fire. There are signs all around asking people to come forward if they saw any odd activity around the toilets about six am on the day of the fire. I didn't see anything like that but was witness to the dense white-grey smoke billowing out of the toilets as I made my way out of the railway station to Nottingham Market Square catch a bus to work.'

'It is eighteen months after the railway station fire incident and in the paper today they say a (named) woman has been sentenced to twenty-five months in prison for starting the fire in the ladies toilet causing £5.6 million worth of damage. She was a drug user and habitual thief who had gone into the toilets to take heroin and crack cocaine. The judge says that her action of discarding the smouldering debris in a plastic waste bin as she left the toilets was a reckless, thoughtless act with complete disregard to the general pubic but not, deliberate arson. He also said that an inquiry into the way the toilets were built regarding fire prevention had revealed them as an accident waiting to happen.'

'Not long after the new Clifton-Toton tram line opened a clever car driver thought it would be quicker to drive their four by four vehicle along the tram line via the Queens Medical Centre. This means driving off the road and up a section of the tram line that goes up, like a roller coaster track, over the busy motorway a hundred plus feet below. Then the track levels out at the QMC tram stop. The tram track continues back downwards to the road. It is clearly not meant for road traffic and, *quelle surprise,* the four by four got stuck*!* The result was that it had to be craned off the track causing hours of delays for tram passengers. Some good did come from this as the self-same incident co-coincided with the invention of the popular abbreviation we now know as ffs.'

'Although I am happy to drink a coffee on the bus or tram I always find myself getting a bit self-conscious regarding eating anything whilst travelling. The nice steaming hot bacon cob that I have purchased *en route* to work ideally needs to be consumed, in my humble cob eating opinion, at the railway station, before I get on any mode of public transport. I suppose part of my thoughts around this are the fact it is difficult to juggle a rucksack, a newspaper, a life-sized model of a benign Stegosaurus, a hot coffee and a yummy bacon and bread based snack whilst trying to find a seat for the journey. Even though I am a polite, closed mouth, type eater I don't want to bother other people with my breakfast habits. And, for the record, I never ever say "Nom noms."

This isn't the case with a fair amount of my fellow travellers on both buses and trams. Many a time my nostrils have been violently assailed with the abominable whiffs of flavoured crisps, hot pizzas, fish and chips doused in a gallon of vinegar, cockles in vinegar, Burger King burgers, pop corn by the sack load, and even curries. As if the smells aren't bad enough, there is the feeling that you have to watch some idiot chowing down on a microwaved scalding hot Cornish pasty. A Cornish pasty that is so scalding hot they are juggling it around their saliva drenched open gobs to evade major tongue and palate burning. But, maybe I am just a food prude.'

'A thankfully rare incident occurred on the homeward bound tram this evening. There was a scruffy old bloke trying to hide the fact he was smoking a home-made roll up on the tram. I could smell a distinct aroma of cigarette smoke in the air and looked over to this guy slumped on one of the tip up seats 'hiding' a fag in his curled up, rather sooty looking hand. As the tram moved down over the University Boulevard part of the track he took a few sly tokes of the forbidden cigarette. He no doubt imagined himself on the *Côte d'Azur* amongst the café frequenting glitterati on fifty *Gauloises* a day and drinking enough wine to pickle a reluctant cow. He fell off the tram three stops later finding himself in the middle of NG2, a kind of office based business no-man's land with lots of shiny blue windows.'

'Another viewing of a well known person today. I know it's only about seven am but I do start to wonder why I am seeing a bespectacled Alan Bennett working as an ordinary bus driver on my daily bus. As I show him my travel card I swear I hear him ask if I have seen his dearly departed friend Thora Hird lately. I think I confused him rather by replying that, alas and alack, I hadn't, but had loved his anecdotal book Keeping On Keeping On. I told him that I particularly enjoyed his stories about the time he was writing the play version of The Wind In The Willows for the National Theatre and, furthermore, the poetic notion that he thought childhood was on ration in the 1940s. We had a lovely conversation. Behind me, a distinctly tetchy lady in a long shabby overcoat looking like a poor man's version of the actress Maggie Smith. She was very impatient to pay her fare. So, I reluctantly took my place amongst the hoi polloi. It's not every day one gets to chat with Alan Bennett on one's bus but Mrs Grumpy Pants didn't seem to appreciate that. The Thora Hird lookalike that followed Mrs Grumpy Pants in the queue brightened my early morning trip considerably. I could feel Alan positively glowing from his bus cab. He thought she was dead.'

'Fly on the tram alert. A big fat, full of maggots, blue bottle type fly has flown on to my tram at the Lace Market stop. I know for a fact it hasn't purchased a ticket (you can just tell – flies aren't subtle). If the ticket inspectors get on at some random stop then the fly is going to be fined fifty pound for not possessing a ticket or having a valid card. These flies think they can get away with it because they are a public nuisance, a bit erm - fly by night. Well, this one is doing the rounds throughout the carriages today showing off its nuisance qualities big time.

First it lands on someone's head, then it spins off and crashes into the window but miraculously survives. On the floor it makes full use of the echo quality of its space and buzzes like a top quality vibrator with brand new batteries. This confuses one of the young lady passengers who, blushing beetroot red, goes rooting through her handbag for her suddenly noisome Greedy Girl Rabbit friend. The fly now vanishes and I start to worry. What if it's lost? What about Mrs Fly back home? And how would the fly kids cope without Daddy fly? What if it bumped into a rough crowd of hover flies or worse, a sticky spider's web!? At the terminal the fly reappears from nowhere and does a victory roll and a smart aerobatic move out of the just closing door.'

'Here is a 'only slightly exaggerated' conversation between two girls on the bus. They are possibly in their late teens. It went thus; "Like literally she said ... and then I says to her like... Honest to God, seriously like. She was then like... and I said like yeah whatevs like... on my life. Oh my days! Like. Literally that's what she like - said, like. Basically, I thought like she can go do one. Like, you know what I'm saying? Like she like so totally goes on one about it all. It was well embarrassing. Like tears and everything. Literally, basically like proper tears like. I have to, like. tell her to, like, fess up and pull yourself like together like. Like you know what I'm saying? Like."

'Not so long after the "Hello!" child (remember him?) came the "Mommy? Can I dwar?" child. It meant draw of course but in child speak it came out a more sickly sounding dwar. Also the word Mommy had a distinctly American twang to it like Marmy. So for yet another half hour journey there was a constant stream of the same questioning except the noun changed on each question. The 'Mommy' was indifferent to the questions and spent pretty much the whole time on her mobile phone whilst the child was asking about being genuinely creative. Albeit, a tad over insistent.

Child: Mommy can I dwar a piggy?

Mother: (on mobile phone) hmm.

Child: Mommy can I dwar a horsey?

Mother: (on mobile phone) hmm.

Child: Mommy can I dwar a kitty?

Mother: (on mobile phone) hmm.

Child: Mommy can I dwar a mommy?

Mother: (on mobile phone) hmm. If you want. Mommy's busy.

Child: Mommy can I dwar the internet?

Mother: (on mobile phone) hmm. Hey?

Child: Mommy can I dwar Daddy's lady friend who comes to see Daddy when you are out?

Mother: (on mobile phone) hmm. If you like. Stop bothering Mommy. What did you just say?

Child: I want to dwar Daddy kissing the nice lady. She lets me dwar.

Overheard comment: "I really love polishing things but only when I don't have to."

'A pigeon is playing dare devil with the bus as it traverses through the pleasant housing estate of Compton Acres on the outskirts of Nottingham tonight. I am sitting on the top deck in the panoramic view front seat. I am looking down as it flies down just feet from the front of the thirty miles an hour moving vehicle. I'm not sure what it is trying to pick up from the road but, each time it disappears from sight my heart leaps up with the dreadful thought that we are going to leave behind a very flat, extremely squished, deader than dead, pigeon.

But no! By some miracle of nature and pigeon good fortune the gods have smiled on this plucky pigeon. Up it majestically shoots again, the soft glow of the setting evening sun giving its wings an almost angelic appearance. Pigeon poetry. It's the best.'

Overheard comment: "I made him a shopping list and definitely put 'Don't get no lamb's liver'. He's bloody useless. He came back with pig's liver instead."

'If I sit upstairs on the bus I am privy to an overhead view of parts of many people's private gardens. At one point I even considered taking photos and making a photo book about awful looking garden spaces. Working title: 'More Chavvy Than Chelsea'. Whilst there are some very nice looking gardens along the merry bus route home, some of the others don't even qualify as garden spaces. They are more like dumping grounds for decades worth of useless crap. The view is more like an unkempt builders' yard than something that might take pride of place on a soft lit Gardener's World programme or win a top prize at the RHS Chelsea Flower Show. I have also witnessed Gnomageddon in a garden that featured several smashed up gnomes scattered about within the sporadic oily grass patches and deeply despairing dandelions. I still have nightmares about that. Call me Mr Sensitive. As for the garden with the giant garden trampoline surrounded by weeks old, fly blown Rottweiler poo and deflated footballs. Well, enough said.'

'Originally this book was going to be called Overheard On Public Transport but after a little consideration I realised that what I was writing was more about what I and my fellow travellers generally saw rather than specifically heard. All that might have changed through, in what I have jokingly called the days of the overused platitudes. These are days when I hear conversations from people who say a lot of things that add nothing to their meaning. These common expressions can be heard all over Britain like lazy linguistic sandwich fillers. Some examples? Sure, at the end of the day, when you think about it, why not?

"At the end of the day. What it all boils down to. When you think about it. It is what it is. What will be will be. Let's agree to disagree. What doesn't kill you makes you stronger. We all have to do things we don't want to do. You gotta do what you gotta do. Everything happens for a reason. When you gotta go you gotta go. When I win the Lottery. It's not rocket science. Don't live in the past. The customer is always right. It's the thought that counts. Hard work never killed anyone. The road to Hell is paved with good intentions." Enough said.'

Overheard comment: "White dog poo? Haven't seen any in years. I wonder if it is to do with Brexit?"

'I was on the midday bus going into Nottingham when a group of young Chinese people got on and quickly went upstairs. One of the young women had a tote bag with the logo message 'Get Over It!' I wanted to ask her what the 'it' was that the world needed to get over. It was so ill defined. 'It' could have referred to anything, couldn't it? Was it Information Technology? If so, surely that should have been I.T. It must have been important and somewhat urgent otherwise there would be no need for the exclamation mark. Was the bag made in the UK or elsewhere? Maybe I overthink these things. Life is confusing when confronted with abstract directions like 'Get Over It!' but – I suppose I will, eventually, get over it.'

Overheard comment: "Musical bloody theatre! To my mind if you've got summat to say you shouldn't have to make a song and dance about it."

'Early one morning, on the tram ride to work, the rising sun was shining through the tram window. It was almost blinding me. The tram stopped and Jesus of Nazareth got on the tram. This was made even more shocking because Easter Sunday had just passed. There he was in all his biblical glory. Jesus was kitted out in old brown, broken backed, M&S sandals, and an off-white full length gown with hood. He had a shaggy salt and pepper beard and long unkempt hair. Jesus stood unsteadily for a few stops whilst me and my fellow passengers gaped open mouthed. Predictably another passenger blurted out "Jesus Christ!" Then he got off and quietly disappeared in the direction of the Holy Spirits off-licence. Our Lord has arisen thought I, but I then realised he was just local eccentric who could hold his liquor and probably had a mother named Mary.'

'My twenty year-old work colleague Milly, is a slightly built pretty girl with bright pink hair and a deep love for flamingos. Today she came in with a black eye. It wasn't caused by a flamingo. It turns out that there was a fight on her bus. The fight was between a woman and a man. Both were drunk and the woman was attacking the man by punching him in his face repeatedly and screaming at him to go away. But not in those actual words. Milly told me that everyone on the bus seemed shocked but did nothing to help the man who was now bleeding badly from the blows. Milly tried to verbally calm the woman down and got herself a smack in the eye for her trouble. Sometimes you don't know if it is a good or bad thing to interfere. The attacking woman grabbed the man's wallet and threw it out of the bus window. Milly got off the bus and never found out how the incident continued.'

Overheard comment: "Is it wrong to find a Disney character sexually attractive?"

'Reading amusing books on public transport can be a good thing to pass the time away and enjoy a smile or two. However, when they are written by great writers like Clive James or Caitlin Moran, Bill Bryson or Helen Fielding there is a great possibility of your smiles quickly developing into a choking fit as you suddenly burst out laughing and terrify the other passengers. Worse still is, if you are combining reading a funny book and drinking at the same time. A fizzy drink abruptly cannoning out of your nose and onto several fellow passengers and the book, is not funny at all. Not even if Bill Bryson, or my humble self has made you laugh.'

Overheard comment: "I think I've got that attention decrepit disorder."

'Being a musical theatre fan and regular theatre reviewer I often have show songs or odd lines on a repeat loop in my head as I travel. These are probably generated in my mind because I am going to see a particular show or have been listening to music at home. I have certain favourites and the freaky thing is that I start to envisage the people I travel alongside as characters from the shows. On certain bus journeys the whole cast from *Les Misérables* can appear. There is sad Fantine with her baby Cosette. Upstairs are the students on the way to the barricades or a local version of the ABC cafe. Javert glowers menacingly at Jean Valjean as, once again he escapes his clutches, this time by jumping off the bus at the wrong stop. Rascally M. Thenardier picks the pockets of any poor unwitting soul standing up and within his thieving grasp. Any moment now the whole ensemble of travellers are going to burst into a thrilling rendition of 'Do You Hear The People Sing?' led by handsome Enjolras, the rebellious bus driver.

I just thank the Lord that I have not manifested the soundtrack to Summer Holiday on to the folk who are travelling with me. I'm not sure how much I could stand the sudden sight of everyone in garish coloured shorts, summery shirts and bikinis going all Sir Cliff Richard on me! Surely passengers hanging out of the bus windows and open door is against health and safety regulations.'

Overheard comment: " I can't wait to get home. I think I've got too much glitter in me knickers."

'A friend who has lived in London for most of her life tells me some grim tales from her journeys in and around the capital and south of the river Thames. She has an Oyster Card and travels both on the underground and the bus. Here is what she has to say.

"Trying to get off the tube train especially at peak times is virtually impossible Phil. The people on the platform wanting to get on just surge on without a thought for others. I have even pretended I am going to be sick and suddenly everyone gets out of my way. In the Summer, on a hot train, other people's body odour, especially the dank underarm bits, can get right into your nostrils. It's a real relief to get off and rush upstairs to the street level to choke on some car fumes instead. I've never seen this next thing, thank God, but one work colleague of mine came into the office looking a bit green. Apparently someone had done an actual shit on the back seat of her bus and she nearly sat in it. That's gross!

I'm going to sound a right misery here Phil but I can't bear it when the buskers get on and start playing to their captured audience. Some are actually good and friendly but, after a hard day at work I just want to do the Londoner thing and put my head down or read for the journey home. I don't like Bob Dylan songs or excerpts from Hamilton sung at me with the suggestion I should tip the musicians, thank you very much. The American crowd in the next carriage would love it I bet. So entertain them, not me. The funny thing is if I was in New York on holiday and it happened on a subway commute there, I'd probably love it. It's all down to context and my mood I guess."

Overheard comment: "I'm not anorexic honest. That lot keep saying I'm anorexic. Seriously though, I eat so much junk food it's unbelievable. Yesterday I actually ate a whole orange!"

'On occasion my bus home from work fills up with sports fans as the route goes over Trent Bridge. Within a few minutes walk either way there are two major football grounds, Nottingham Forest and Notts County. For fans of cricket local and international there is the Trent Bridge Cricket Ground. There are also the, lesser known, Nottingham Naked Chess Players Club and West Bridgford Humane Grey Squirrel Jugglers Society.

Last July, both the chess playing and squirrel juggling groups had their members banned from the bus services following a bust up on the top deck of the number six bus. One of the grey squirrel jugglers insisted on taking his best pair of live squirrels upstairs in a flimsy cardboard carrying case. Both hungry squirrels escaped out of the box and became gruesomely entangled with an elderly naked chess player protecting his precious antique pieces in his lap. The whole X rated incident was captured on CCTV and the squirrels were unharmed. The larger of the two squirrels said, through an interpreter, that after a hard day of being gently juggled he was just after some juicy nuts.

However, back in reality land, we travellers do encounter the football fans who pack the bus to the gills. They are generally well behaved and are mostly men and boys. The Forest lot spend the journey moaning about their team not winning and impress each other with an unbelievable step by step, kick by kick, twist and turn, tackle and tickle verbal recount, in minute detail of some vastly overpaid footballer, nearly scoring a goal. How they remember things in such detail is quite beyond me.

The cricket fans are noisier and wear funny feathery headdresses or hats suitable for the Australian outback. They talk about sticky wickets, the inclement weather and have unfathomable conversations concerning weird rules and random numbers and hitting balls for four. Whatever that means.'

Overheard comment: "The new boss started today. He's about three foot tall and looks about twelve. Can't see him lasting long, can you?"

'Sometimes it is possible to start a bus or tram journey with the self knowledge that you need to go to the loo quite urgently. Even so, you board the public transport, take a seat and hope to God you don't have a publicly shaming accident *en route*.

Occasionally this has happened to me and I've been lucky to be able to jump off and find a toilet quickly. This is usually where there is a friendly pub or café nearby. But what do you do when you are in a foreign land and find yourself with a sudden case of being aware that you need to get to the loo pretty darn quick? Just to be clear we are not talking about a wee. It is an awful feeing in your stomach as the back door trots, the thunder down under, the Deli belly or the runs loom frighteningly large and unavoidable.

A couple of years ago I was in *Bordeaux* on holiday on my own. During a hot and sunny day I had been exploring this beautiful French city. I had gone quite a way out by tram and foot into the suburb of *St Michel* and its famous flea market. I was enjoying taking some photos of the old buildings and attractions when I felt, in my gut, that I should start heading back fairly rapidly in order to find a toilet facility.

An earlier meal containing quite a lot of roughage including prunes, washed down with a cold beer or three, was determined to make an accelerated way through my intestines and painfully squirt out the other end. That wasn't too much detail for you, was it?

More urgent gurgling was taking place as I walked in trepidation towards the brown flowing river *Garonne* to hopefully connect with the quick arrival of a city centre bound tram. Ten perilous minutes later, one arrived at the *St-Michel* tram stop and we surged onwards towards the end stop at *Quinconces*. I say 'surged' and that word implies speed. The reality was, as the tram slowly snaked down various riverside quays, the *quai des Salinaires*, the *quai Richelieu* and *quai de la Douane*, we leisurely stopped at the *porte de Bourgogne,* and *place de la Bourse*. I didn't know the French for hurry up. Not that it would have done me any good. Finally, after ten to fifteen minutes more of leg crossing hell the tram terminated at the last stop called *Quinconces*.

I had barely taken a breath throughout the whole nerve racking tram journey because, if I dared to be so foolish, I imagined I would unleash the squity demons of my oh so delicate *derrière*.

I now had some half-familiar streets to navigate to get back to my bijou hotel in the *Chartons* district and the blessed relief of a toilet. Every few feet I would come to a sudden halt as I stood like a startled statue and felt myself going hot and cold as I crossed my legs tightly and fervently wished the feeling of shitting oneself, away.

Two more feet. The same. Three more feet. The same. Some toilets in the actual street were locked and the potential toilets in the Contemporary Art Gallery were too risky to hunt down. Crossing any road was like some crazy dare devil game with no chances to stop safely and stare into the void. Eventually, I got on the home run and, painfully slowly, I edged my way to my hotel at the far end of the *rue Notre Dame*. Anyone seeing me standing and staring ardently up into the air would have imagined I had a deep interest in rustic French roof tiles.

My hotel was open. Thanking all the French saints and their devotees I finally made it up to my room on the second floor. Struggling to get the key to turn in the lock I mentally pleaded with it to turn. With a sudden snapping sound, it did. My rapid entrance into the dark bathroom was quicker than I ever thought I could move. If there was an Olympic medal for trouser dropping I was a gold medal winner. The rest was just sheer relief at finishing the bum holding challenge without a grievous mishap.'

Overheard comment: "I can't remember exactly what it was called but it was something, something, something … anus."

'I've often missed a bus stop because I have been engrossed in a newspaper article or theatre programme. The latter has occurred when I've been out to review something at the theatre and I'm returning home and mentally preparing to draft my review. I've got onto the bus in Nottingham city centre and opened the programme. Periodically, I've glanced up and recognised a couple of the stops coming out of the city centre past the railway station. Then I've got lost in the words of the programme. This type of journey would take around twenty-five minutes and the next thing you know my bus would be sailing past my stop. Luckily for me the next stop is just around the corner. Imagine if it was miles away and I had to walk all the way back!'

Overheard comment: Retired woman to me. "My son always says to trust no-one. There's no point in giving people chances because they just take advantage and throw it back in your face."

'I live in a large village surrounded by two housing estates. The route in and out of the village is serviced by very regular stops until the bus gets to the main road heading towards Nottingham. The walk into the housing estates would take less than ten minutes even for a slow paced person. Yet I have seen people who live on these housing estates wait at the bus shelter for the next bus, for up to half an hour, jump on and then get off two stops down. Idleness, doesn't even begin to describe it.'

Overheard comment: "Why would I want a trainee doctor messing around inside me? I wouldn't even go to a trainee hairdresser!"

'Too often we see people on public transport with their feet up on the seats in front of them. It is awkward to be confrontational and ask/tell them to get their feet down and that other people have got sit there. Even more awkward is when the offender, as we shall call them, has no shoes on, and put their bare feet on the seat. Taking it one step further, many of us still say nothing (well, we might huff and tut a bit) if the person then starts to clip their toenails! Where does it end? Pants down and start trimming their bush with the kitchen scissors? Well, a positive slant would be that it would save time not having to do it in a work break by the water cooler.

On the same theme, I did read a story online recently about an older man travelling on the Tube (London Underground) who asked a kid to get his feet off the seat next to him so that he could sit down. The kid just gave him a sullen look and ignored the older man. He guy asked again. Once more the boy gave the man a 'fuck you' look and ignored his polite request. So the guy just sat on the boy's legs! Apparently the kid looked totally shocked to have an eighteen stone man land on his legs and the rest of the passengers burst into applause!'

'Over time I have learnt a valuable lesson in bus travel etiquette. Instead of just assuming that the other people in a bus queue are getting the same destination bus as me, I now ask. Why? Because in the past I have assumed that the people ahead of me are hoping to get the same bus as me and I've patiently waited until they stick their hand out only to watch my bus go sailing by. It's so frustrating when several buses operate from the same stop!'

'A baby on my bus is crying like a whining early Sunday morning hedge trimmer. It hasn't stopped for twenty minutes and now the evil demon inside me is wanting to push the oblivious parent and baby duo off the bus mid stop. Sometimes I wish I had attended Hogwarts so that I had a handy wand and spell to perform my demonic deed.'

Overheard comment: Old chap. "She said I'm just a dirty old man. I said I'm not at all - them days are over."

'There's a young twenty-something mother in the seat in front of me getting annoyed at her young son. He looks like a cheeky two to three year-old. He's wearing reigns featuring the Teenage Mutant Ninja Turtles. He keeps answering her back. Twice now she's told him to sit down but he gives her his best Mutant Ninja Turtle defiant look. "Sit down now." she says. "You sit down NOW or I will put jam on the back of your legs!" He looks most anxious and immediately sits. The kid is completely silent for the rest of the journey. It makes you wonder why this frightened him. Did she once put jam on the back of his legs and set a swarm of furious jam loving bees upon him? Will he grow up to have a phobia about jam products? And bees.'

Overheard comment: "And, I went to try and help somebody in the shop, like you do, and the new boss woman said that we don't help people – we are just here to serve."

'Two women and a man are discussing weddings and one of the women pipes up "Do you know what the average price is for a wedding nowadays? £17000! Who'd pay that for a ruddy wedding?" Second woman says "Not me." A male companion adds his opinion. "I'd pay no more than £10 to get wed and I might treat her to a bag of chips, as well."

'If the average cocaine addict uses 6mg of cocaine a day then the bloke behind me must be averaging around a kilo a day. Sniff sniff sniff sniff sniff sniff sniff sniff sniff sniff sniff sniff sniff sniff sniff sniff sniff cough sniff sniff sniff sniff sniff. I'm finding myself sniffing along with him. Now we are into alternative sniffing. He sniff me sniff he sniff me sniff. He's getting off the tram now and gives one last sniff as the doors open.'

'A woman next to me on the bus related this tale. "Then the bus driver stopped where she shouldn't. She picked up this gay lad who'd obviously been out on the lash with his pretend girlfriend. It was a bloody nightmare. It's Sunday morning and he's shrieking like a camp queen. He wouldn't shut up! All drama queen and no let up. He was going "Oh you are the best driver! Seriously the best! You really are! What's your name?

I'm going to tell Trent Barton. You are like THE best! An a.n.g.e.l. Not kidding. Seriously! An angel. Oh my God! Seriously – you're the best! Oh my God! I thought like I would be well narked if we'd not got this bus. You are just the best! Honestly! The best. Seriously." Me and another woman got off two stops early because we couldn't stand hearing him going on. His 'girl' friend was just as bad. Both of 'em as high as kites."

'I see a young mother and I am not sure if the child with her is a boy or girl. Mother and child chat normally at the bus shelter and get on the bus. The name of the child is Charlie or Charleee as the mother says it. We hear this expanded name what seems like a thousand times on the journey. "Look Charleee that's where mummy works. Are we on the bus Charleee? No Charleee, I'm the adult. Do as I say Charleee. Sit still Charleee. Going round a corner now Charleee. Hang on now Charlee. Weeh, that's good isn't it Charleee? On the bus Charleee. We are on the bus. When we get to town Charlee, we're getting the number 36 Charleee. Going to see daddy, aren't we Charleee?

Charlie just responds by either saying bus with a very hissy s sound or by cackling loudly like an evil child from a horror film. Coming to a cinema near you this Autumn – Charleee. Certificate X'

Overheard comment: Old man reading some signage on the bus word for word out loud. "Ultra low emission zone. These buses feature stop - start technology. Stop - start technology? What the f**k is that all about?"

'This is twice in the last couple of days that the person behind me on the bus has mistaken my head for the back of the seat and levered themselves up by pressing down on my head. Note to self: I must change the design on my wool hat. Clearly it blends in too well with the bus furniture. Another thing I have noticed as well is people in the seat behind sliding their hand and part of their forearm through the gap between seat and window thus encroaching on my personal space. I'm thinking of carrying a super sharp needle with me so I can stab the offender's hand and send it scurrying back to where it should be. Wouldn't that be fun boys and girls?'

'Today it is raining cats and dogs and therefore I am fully expecting the scourge of the umbrella shakers to appear. These are fellow passengers who have protected themselves from the rain by using an umbrella. Fair enough. However, when they get on the bus they neglect to shake the drops of rain water from the umbrella outside. Realising their mistake they go towards an empty seat shaking the wet umbrella on the legs of those already seated. There should be a kind of revenge shower unit built into the bus that soaks the offenders but doesn't splash anyone else.'

Overheard comment: Irritated woman to nail clipper. "Right! Whoever it is clipping their nails the whole bus can hear you! So bloody stop now. That's them told."

'On public transport there are space facilities for baby buggies and that's good because, even with a safety belt, tethering a buggy and its baby occupant to the back of a speeding tram or bus is just going to lead to trouble, isn't it now?

This very morning I was sat next to a toddler wagon and took the personally unusual step of waving at the baby. You may get the impression that I don't like babies from previous stories. I do, just not the noisy ones. The baby smiled back at me then turned into the baby of a thousand faces. Up went the eyebrows to indicate deep puzzlement about this person who is not daddy waving at him. Then, a quite baffling range of expressions flickered across this baby's face like an emotional time lapse film. Happy, sad, puzzlement, accusative, plain weird, mouth down on one side, then the other, a pouting face and next a sudden look to the mother completed by bubble blowing with its saliva. As the infant face went bright red and a facial sense of nappy filling was expressed I suddenly saw an invisible, child free, adult friend further down the carriage.'

Overheard comment: Middle-aged woman to her friend. "So I am sitting in the kitchen looking out into the garden and he's back. The robin. He's sitting on the seat that we got from granddad when he passed away. I'd just been thinking about him and there's that robin again. I swear it's granddad come back in the shape of a robin to tell us he is well. The way it moves its head it is just like granddad when he had one of his cricks in the neck. Honesty. Bet you think I'm daft, don't you?" Friend says "No. Not at all. My husband Jack came back as a thrush. Which is funny because he used to get thrush a lot before he met me. The bird used to dance on the birdbath whenever I put the radio on. If Abba was playing it would fly away. Jack never liked Abba. That thrush had to be him. Just had to be!"

'Sometimes when you hear people wrongly pronouncing a word it can make you smile. Other times you want to boldly stand up from your seat and put them right. One day I overheard a middle-aged woman talking to her friend about horror films. Apparently she didn't like the modern horror films as they were far too scary. "I used to like them 'ammer 'orror films – Peter Cushion and Christopher Leak." she said. The next ten minutes were thrillingly filled with her love of Dracula. Except she didn't say Dracula. The name came out as Dracleea and apparently, when he got 'kilt' by Peter Cushion, his body became a skellington and then it was dust. No doubt he was kilt with a steak. Frankingstein never got mentioned.'

Overheard comment. Elderly chap on the tram speaking loudly on his mobile about his food experience in hospital. "Hello! Can you hear me? Can you HEAR me? I've just got out. Ospikal. Been in ospikal. Long time. Fell over. Nearly broke every bone in me body. On the way back now. No, I'm not hungry. Had summat at ospikal. I had baked beans in a plastic cup, hash browns, fried egg, bacon and cheap sausages. Then a yoghurty thing. Yesterday was better. I ate shepherd's pie with gravy and mixed vegetables. Cleaned me plate up. Like a good boy. You can't hear me? I SAID I've been in ospikal... (repeats the whole thing again and then belches) … that'll be them cheap sausages."

'It appears that sometimes when I am on public transport, including today, I have a big - visible only to the rude people – sign over my head that says that I have no clue what I am doing. The tram pulls up at my stop and I press the light up button on the doors to let me and those behind me, get off. Nothing happens so I press it again. Some grumpy arsed bloke behind grunts "ffs" under his coffee and fags breath except he uses the full words, with a high degree of venom. He virtually pushes in front of me so he can jab at the button himself with his superior fat finger. The doors open and, because he is so important, he finds it imperative to squeeze himself out of the doors ahead of me. As he grumps off I hear him say "Not ruddy rocket science!" Charming. Upon disembarking, I notice that there is a bag left on one of the seats. Is it too evil to hope that it belonged to him?'

'I was sat in a bus shelter at Nottingham railway station and the only other people sat next to me were a small boy and an older man. I made an assumption based on grey hair and wrinkles that the older man was the boy's granddad. The sun was very hot and the granddad put the boy into the relative shade and started to tell him a story out loud. The story was built up of short and simple sentences and it went something like this. "Once upon a time there was a big whale. The whale lived right at the bottom of the sea. He loved living there because it was dark. He didn't use his eyes very much. He didn't need to, in the dark. He was the biggest fish in the sea. All day long he swam around eating anything like insects and plankton and seaweed and other smaller fish. Even the sharks were afraid of him. Because it was so dark - not even humans went down to where the whale lived. But one day the whale saw a very bright light which nearly blinded him and something hard then bonked him on top of his head..."

My bus appeared at the end of the road and I got up to put my arm out. As the bus got nearer I turned to the granddad and jokingly asked him to email me the rest of the story. He looked a bit shocked that a stranger had spoken to him. I mean, the nerve of me doing that. Then he smiled and said that he couldn't do that because it was copyrighted and anyway, he was making it up as he went along. Amused, I jumped on my bus and contemplated what the bright light was and what had bonked the whale on the head. I will never know. One thing I do know is that I bet the granddad never thought I'd write all this down.'

Overheard comment: "I can't stand that Jamie Oliver. He eats with his mouth open and he looks like a slobbering bloated bear with a carrot up its arse. Give me the Two Hairy Bikers anytime."

'Oh dear. Oh deary deary me. The big scary 'care in the community' man has just come down to the lower deck on the bus in his shorts and grubby tee-shirt which features the logo 'Hug Me Tight! I'm Your Friend.' The guy is dangling from the support straps opposite me like a gorilla whose forgotten his medication. I just want to go home with my bag of food. I really do. I am five stops away. It is very hot today and the fifteen stone, unpredictable scary man, who introduces himself to everyone as Bob, is being very loud about his personal sweat. He says - no bellows - "Hello I'm Bob! What're your names? I'm sweating! Sweating a lot. The sweat is pouring down my back!" I try not to imagine this, but fail badly.

Bob repeats this many times as if fellow passengers haven't quite grasped his dilemma. "Where are you going?" he demands of a woman getting off the bus as quickly as she can. He continues relentlessly on his sweaty discourse. "I'm sweating. I'm sticky all over. Everything is sticking to me. The sweat is running down my bum crack!"

I am most definitely trying to get the sweaty bum crack image out of my head now. I fail again. Even more badly than before. "Are you all hot and sweaty? I am!" he enquires of the few remaining passengers.

One woman finally answers him by telling him that, actually, it is hot for everyone. At this point he thrusts his hand into his shorts pocket and frantically plays pocket billiards. Oh the total *joy* of travelling on public transport.'

Overheard comment: "We were going to have a barbecue yesterday but all the sausages were burnt black and tasted too much of petrol."

'A very common topic of conversation on British public transport is – you've guessed it – the weather. It has been said that we moan about the weather, on and off, an average of two hours a day. We love to have a moan about it being too hot, too cold, too muggy, too much snow or too much rain. I often overhear people complaining that the weather is so unpredictable and that you can never trust the weather forecasters. It is said, that we like moaning about the weather because, it makes us feel better. Yet there is a division over whether discussing the weather is actually interesting. It is claimed that weather talk is a kind of social code that we have evolved to help us overcome social inhibitions and actually talk to one another, especially strangers. How scientific.

One of the things that causes the most contention is if the topic of what the weather is doing today, is disputed. Failing to agree with the other person's weather opinion is considered a real social no no. For example: you are sitting on a bus next to a stranger and it is raining outside. Then, as a sort of a rainy day icebreaker you said something like, "Well, at least its good for the gardens..." and the listener then replied "Really? I don't think the gardens would benefit at all." instantly there would be a frosty moment in the weather topic pleasantries.

Just imagine, on a hotter day, what would happen if you confided to the stranger, sat next to you, that you felt the clammy weather meant it was too hot to have a wank! "Oh yes you are spot on there." the stranger would say, with a knowing smile and a hot hand placed on your upper thigh, "I too found that to be the case earlier. I just went off the boil."

The weather topic tends to make people exaggerate. People say stupid things like "It has been raining for eleven years now." or "When I was a child every single day in the Summer, without fail, was gloriously sunny. We had non-stop picnics in the park and every year, at Christmas, the snow was almost half way up the house. We had to get in and out through the bedroom window and a makeshift slide made of Weetabix. I tell you what though, the schools didn't close, not like nowadays. On no, we were tough. We sat in the class in our 1950s style overcoats, home-knitted wool hats and mittens and our galoshes. Kids today don't know cold. The frost on our eyelashes used to take a week to melt and we just laughed it off as par for the course."

We also tend to laugh at our British weather patterns. It wouldn't be out of place to say that we can be wrapped up against the elements on Saturday, out in our shorts and tee shirts on the Sunday and drenched in a downpour on the Monday.

The wet weather gives us great opportunities to pepper our conversations with idioms and sayings we have grown up with like; it is raining cats and dogs, it never rains but it pours, and the rain's alright for ducks or the garden. Sometimes we speak of saving for a rainy day but given that people tend to stay indoors when it rains I'm not sure how their savings can be utilised on such specific days. Internet shopping perhaps. What is really meant by us saying that we are - right as rain? Allegedly we can make hay when the sun shines but, be honest, how many of us have proper hard graft experience in rural agriculture? Personally, I don't have the foggiest about it but maybe I have my head in the clouds and I wouldn't like to rain on other people's parades, come rain or shine. What a wit!

One thing that often unifies the majority of travellers on the bus, tram or train is seeing the lobster-red exposed body parts of unfortunate men and women who have clearly overdone it in the baking hot sun without wearing any suntan lotion. As they sit around us, glowing like the very fires of Hell, it is possible to imagine a bus load of thought bubbles hovering over the other passengers. In the thought bubbles we can read things like 'Ouch that must really sting.', 'What do they look like?' and 'It's April you idiot. Don't you know that you never cast a clout until May is out!?' Clearly not.

Just don't get people started on the subject of snow. This icy weather condition is well known for dividing opinion. The complaints, just like a snowy downpour, come thick and fast. If there is too little the kids can't go tobogganing. They still try anyway and ruin the grass. If there is above one inch of snow, chaos reigns in the UK and all the schools have to close by law. The County Councils seem totally unprepared. It is like the very idea or event of snow in Winter is a massive surprise to them. There is never enough gritting done. The new word snowmageddon is bandied about as soon as we spy one tiny snowflake floating down.

Newspapers across the country go mad with dramatic warnings and pepper their metrological journalism with exclamation marks!!!!! Headlines are dragged out from the year before like they have been sitting in a lexi-freezer. 'Going Snowhere!', 'UK faces coldest winter on record!', 'Britain braced for snow and ice hell', 'Travel misery as cold weather continues', 'Percy the Penguin at London Zoo loves it!', and 'Canadians and

Finlanders chortle as Brits struggle under one inch of snow.' The newspaper snow stories are littered with words like havoc, disorder, disarray, confusion, mayhem, turmoil, shambles and mess. When it gets properly deep and covers everything over we say it looks pretty on Christmas cards or okay if we don't have to venture out in it. Otherwise we are glad when it all melts. Unless you are Percy the penguin at London Zoo.

For those people who don't like their jobs, they pray fervently to the weather gods to make the snowy conditions so severe that it is impossible to turn up for work even on skis or those snow shoes they paid two quid for at a car boot sale. But for young people who like to go clubbing and boozing around town it is perfectly alright to wear as little as possible in the snow, ice and slush and well below freezing temperatures. Magaluf style flip flops are deemed okay footwear in the snow and ice. They are young, hot-blooded and enjoy half drunk visits to the hospital where they are treated for hypothermia and utter foolhardiness.'

Overheard Comment: "In this hot weather the clothes I wear are based on how obvious my sweat stains will be."

'I got off the bus yesterday to be confronted by a large teddy bear abandoned by the park railings. The ground on which it was sitting was a mess of dog pee grass and cigarette butts. The forlorn looking bear had one eye missing. The remaining one was white with a rich red background like a shattered glass of full bodied red wine. Its arms were outstretched like it was super desperate for a loving hug and it displayed a world weary attitude borne about by being left in the rain for weeks. If it could speak its vocabulary would be festooned with bitter expletives. The middle white tummy section was filthy and next to the bear was an abandoned and crushed tin of Special Brew. Life can be cruel.'

Overheard comment: "It's ridiculous. As soon as he has decorated one room his wife says the rest of the house now looks in need of doing. Then she immediately makes him decorate the rest. I think divorce might be on the cards. It's an endless circle of decorating and apparently, they haven't had sex in months."

'Opposite me is a very defensive and opinionated older man. I am guessing mid seventies in age. All his clothes look charity shop shabby but definitely not shabby chic. His apparel includes a grubby red peaked baseball cap. He's wearing a striped blazer that has fond memories of when the buttons and button holes didn't play a valiant but fruitless tug of war over the vast void of his beer belly. On the lapels of the jacket are pinned nineteen enamel trophy badges. Three of them feature Union Jack flags and the rest are connected to bus spotting. His Robertsons' Jam Golliwog figure on a motor racing bike stands out as being a bit odd amongst the bus related collection. Pride of place is a public service vehicle conductor badge (green trim and white interior) displaying the identity FF 22374. At his home I have no doubt that there are several decomposing dead bus conductors sporting their 1960s uniforms. Also, there are multiple piles of fusty documentation relating to bus routes and carefully recorded appraisals of the new liveries of the bus world.

Much of his valuable retirement time will have been spent outdoors with his handy notepad, camera and camcorder capturing fleet numbers and *ad hoc* public transport advertisements. It is unlikely this particular one is a bus preservationist because even the most tolerant of his anorak friends would find his negative and belligerent attitudes too much. I was only in his dubious company for ten minutes and that was plenty.

The top pocket of his jacket is sagging under the weight of a baker's dozen of silver topped biros. His hairstyle is retro 1970s and the original silver fox sideburns still sit complacently fluffy either side of his square jawed face. One has a bit of stale cheese in it. A 'know all' look resides behind his rectangular framed glasses. On each little finger of his gargantuan ex-boxer hands he wears matching silver rings. On two Wednesdays a month he gives a grouchy thirty minute talk on old Nottingham- Derby bus routes to the Women's Institute. Sometimes, if he is feeling a bit devilish, he gives them his 'Bus conductors who fiddled the books' talk.'

Overheard comment: Two old ladies talking. First old lady to the other who remains silent. "You never see lamb chops out and about in shops on the high street these days do you?" I think they were referring to supermarket meat shelves especially in the smaller branches. But, on hearing this comment, my imagination went haywire imagining exquisitely dressed lamb chops sauntering arm in arm down the high street like wealthy French *flâneurs* parading about purely to be seen as lamb chops with a life of leisure. They do exist you know.'

'Things get dumped in all sorts of places. Whilst waiting for the tram, very early this morning, I saw a used Russell Hobbs toaster occupying a tram stop seat. Who would bring a toaster to the city centre and why leave it on a tram stop seat? Maybe it was a gift for a friend and it got left there by accident as the purveyor got distracted and boarded the tram. I can almost imagine a slow motion look of horror as the tram departed at speed and the discarded toaster became smaller and smaller until it was just a distant toasting memory in the mind and heart of its owner. Or maybe someone just casually dumped it there because their bin was full. The jury is out on that one until a full police enquiry is concluded by the abandoned objects department. When they find out who it was that left it there - they are toast.'

Overheard comment: "I often wonder what it would be like if people behaved like dogs. You know like barking at each other in the street, sniffing each other's bums, howling and peeing against the wall. Actually some people do all of that! I've watched 'em on Channel Five."

'You don't often see that many very well dressed people on public transport but, the other day I spotted a man dressed in a long, very expensive looking winter coat, a nice quality hat, a buttercup yellow scarf and sharply pressed grey trousers. His black pointy toe shoes were polished within an inch of their lives. Looking closer, as one does, he appeared to have scratched the side of his head near the right ear. The wound looked recent. It was like seeing someone from the 1950s suddenly come to life on our streets and disappear on the number fifty-four bus. Maybe he was a gentleman time traveller.'

'The tram is delayed today. Now that I am finally on it, I am distracted by the man opposite me who is wearing a black padded lightweight jacket that seem to be all the rage at the moment. He's transfixed by his mobile phone. He keeps staring at the screen like something might pop out any second. At the same time he is pinching his nose very firmly with three of his fingers and his thumb. He's been doing this for about ten minutes now and I'm starting to wonder whether, if he lets go, his nose will fall off.'

'There's a woman at the bus stop who is frozen in time. She doesn't move an inch but holds her red mittened hand up to her comically quizzical face which is tilted in the direction of an oncoming tram that has just come into view. She is wearing an over-sized zipped up grey jacket that has a U.S Air Force badge sewn into the design. Given her vacant look I truly hope she isn't flying for them. The tram arrives. I get on and she remains on the platform still in the frozen position. Maybe she is waiting for a fighter jet to land.'

Overheard comment: "It's nearly the end of June and I am still in my winter coat. I pay my taxes. We should get better weather than this, surely."

'I occasionally feel sorry for the carers of others especially those who are forced to push their spouse around in a wheelchair. Invariably the wheelchair user is hugely overweight and the skinny and weary pusher seems to be on their last legs. One pair got on the bus the other afternoon. As well as trying to manipulate the wheelchair and its female occupant onto the bus, the couple had a separate challenge. The bus was jerking about and the woman asked the man to apply her lipstick for her. Several botched attempts later and, after the face saving salvation of some handy wet wipes, he gave up. When she wasn't looking he threw the lipstick in a bin.'

Overheard comment: One woman to another discussing fitness. "Exercise!? Bugger that. The most exercise I do is a walk to the paper shop for a big bar of chocolate."

'It's beyond rare that you get to hear the early songs of Elvis Presley whilst waiting for a tram. However, courtesy of Dads Taxi, (minus apostrophe) I was deafened by Jail-house Rock, That's Alright (Mama), and I Don't Care If The Sun Don't Shine this morning. The last one was quite appropriate as it was starting to rain. Who was Dads Taxi? I will tell you. Dads Taxi was the golden yellow number plate on the front of an old chap's red mobility scooter. He clearly loved Elvis so much he wanted to share the King's sound with most of the town, such was the ear blasting level he played his music at. Yet, when the old fellow drove onto the tram he kindly switched off his music. The occupant of Dads Taxi then spent the journey into Nottingham glowering and All Shook Up at a young man whose choice of music playing on his iPlayer clearly wasn't a patch on Elvis.'

Overheard comment: "She wanted to go to the Opera. No way. From what I've heard it takes them half an hour just sing 'hello'. Come on now! That's wasting valuable drinking time."

'Those who regularly travel on pubic transport will very likely have come across the type known as a Chatty Cathy. Chatty Cathy befriends you at some point on a commute and is – well – far too chatty. She will tell you all sorts of cringe-worthy personal details about her life and family and expects the same level of intimate conversation back from you. Her menstrual cycle isn't an out of bounds topic. But, if you listen carefully you won't hear her talk about her friends, just people and clients at her office. This is because she has no friends. Bare in mind that you are virtually strangers to each other at this point. Alas, Chatty Cathy will instantly turn you into her best mate and turn up on virtually all of your future bus journeys. It's freaky how you have never encountered her before but alas she is now your very own, far too friendly, local stalker.

The only way to get rid of her is to be blatantly rude to her, or categorically refuse to speak. Of course the refusal to speak can be read as there is something wrong with you. This can result in a barrage of *faux* concerned questions. "Are you alright? What's the matter? It isn't something I said, is it?" Throwing a bin bag or dustbin over your own head doesn't help get rid of her either. In fact, such bizarre actions draw even more attention to you as just another weirdo traveller.

I had a Chatty Cathy of my very own. Oh lucky me. We got chatting one day at the village bus stop. Before you could say "Mind your own bloody business." she was asking me how much money I earned and telling me, her ardent listener, that she was only on 40K a year plus expenses and was really struggling. Poor her. She confessed she'd had to cut down her posh restaurant visits to three times a week.

Sporting her eternally sickening grin, I heard endless stories about her kids and her long-suffering husband. Demonstrating her patronising attitudes to the max she fully honed her skill for talking over me whenever I attempted to speak. I came to dread seeing her approach me on a bus and plonk her fat arse next to me with a cheery "Hello mate! You look a bit fed up today. Wossup mate?" Eventually, she told me that her perfect family were moving away to the Outer Hebrides. Sadly, I wouldn't have the pleasure of her cheery 'cheer up mate' chatter any more. I think that was the happiest day of my life. To think just the day before I'd purchased an extra large body bag to hide myself in should she ever turn up on the bus again. Then a few days later she re-appeared at the railway station just when I wasn't expecting her. "Hello mate!" quoth she "Glad I've seen you. We're all off to Scotland now. You look a bit fed up. If you ever fancy a cheap holiday do get in touch. It was always lovely chatting to you."

Overheard comment: On mobile phone. "Go away! All you do is poison me and waste my time!"

'If you are ever of the impression that the British aren't very polite then listen out, as I did the other day, for what people say to the driver as they get off the bus. A young German friend of mine, who was visiting Nottingham, was puzzled that passengers were so vocally grateful for the ride even though they had paid a fare. His opinion was that in Germany the transport has to be exactly on time so there was literally no time for pleasantries with the driver on the bus. I'm not sure how true this is but we Brits love to thank the driver. We say "Thanks driver... cheers... cheers buddy … cheers bud... thanks a lot... cheers mate... thanks - see ya... appreciated... thanks – bye and ta duck. Some young people call the bus driver, drives and drive, without the last r as in … cheers drive/s."

Overheard comment: "She's got an appointment at the doctors. She's got something green and nasty growing in her ears."

'Lots of public transport travellers' gazes tend either to be directed at their mobile phone, out of the window, or at their feet. Sometimes we cannot help noticing other people's shoe attire and today was no exception. No, we are not talking the bright and colourful shoe laces of the young or of flimsy ballet pumps worn in the snow. On this occasion it was an old chap's sandals. They were quite simple in design and moreover what struck me was that he was wearing one blue sock and one brown sock. He was sat with a lady that I assumed was his wife. I desperately wanted to have a joke with them about the odd socks situation but they didn't look like the kind of people who would appreciate my humour at his expense. Maybe, his choice of odd socks was deliberate and a way of his rebelling against pensioner society. Perhaps, he only had two pair of socks and had put the wrong pairing in the washing machine leaving the only option of wearing odd socks and hoping nobody noticed. Peradventure, his wife made him wear them as some kind of kinky fetish or punishment for not mowing the lawn properly. Maybe he was a radical and just didn't care! Yeah! Sock it to 'em old chappie.'

'I don't know why I think that the man I am about to describe is South African. I think it is the 'I'm just off to forage in the veldt for a couple of months dear' tough guy outdoors outfit he wears. Or it could be that his drunk on brandy mumblings, sound like incoherent Afrikaans. Anyway, it is often my displeasure to witness the drama of this huge bloke dressed in well-used jungle boots, canvas cargo pants with strong pockets on the legs for secreting bottles of brandy, or a small Impala deer, and his sebaceous collared, tatty flack jacket. He has very beefy hands with massive 'hard man' rings on most of his fingers. A strong loop of wire goes from his right hand wrist to an ancient carrier bag whose contents clink a lot as he sways on the bus.

As he is so pissed, it takes him quite a while to get on the bus. Then he goes and stands (well, wobbles) in the tip up seat area that is usually dedicated to pushchairs. Only two or three stops later he slowly and awkwardly staggers off the bus again and virtually falls into the wall opposite as he tries to find his feet. As the bus pulls off you can see him clinging on to the chest high wall as he tries to fathom out where the hell he is through the confused fog of his alcohol drenched perceptions. One time

I even saw him wet himself on the bus. He seemed to have no recognition of the deep wet stain starting at the Drakensburg mountain region of his groin widening and lengthening down his cargo pants on to the floor of the bus where it formed a puddle like the beginnings of South Africa's Orange river.'

'It is often nice to see friends on one's bus. Plus, if you haven't seen them for a while, you can engage in a friendly chit chat on the journey. Sometimes though, you see a person you haven't seen for a long while and, in recognising you, they perch themselves down next to you. For some reason they are grinning. In the back of your mind you are trying to figure out why you haven't seen this person. Perhaps you have even blanked their name out of your subconscious.

Then, as they open their mouth to speak, it all comes flooding back like acid reflux. You have deliberately avoided them because all they talk about is their complete obsession with the 1987 cult film *Withnail and I*. Just to prove it, the very first question they ask is not about your health, wealth, job status or growing Welsh thimble collection but... you've guessed it: "Have you seen *Withnail and I* lately?"

Without even waiting for an answer they get great joy in telling you they watched it for the 1151st time on DVD yesterday evening. Despite your look of horror combined with blankness (not an easy action to achieve simultaneously) they verbally drag out every single line of comedy from the film for your, and the whole bus load of passengers' amusement. The dramatically acted out selections of script include "We want the finest wines available to humanity!", "I feel like a pig shat in my head", and "I don't advise a haircut man. All hairdressers are in the employment of the government. Hairs are your aerials..."

Over a hundred quotes flood from his constantly grinning mouth. Believe me when I say that there are truly this many. To prove it, this friend knows every single line backwards and repeats them all at full volume. Its not so much embarrassing, as completely mortifying, when his best camp Uncle Monty quote echoes around the bus. I'll leave you with his fully amplified and wildly gesticulated "You beastly little parasite how dare you!? You little thug how dare you!? Aaargh, you beastly ungrateful little swine!" ringing in your ears.

I got off four stops early to get away from him and he followed me as far as his damned quotes would carry him. When he reached the end of the film script he just started all over. I looked at my watch to see how late my actions had made me. It had stopped and I thought a.k.a *Withnail and I* "Even a stopped clock tells the right time twice a day." Maybe I should go on holiday by mistake.'

'Although nothing has been officially advertised, I am convinced, from the aural evidence of my return bus and tram journey today, that today is actually National Onomatopoeia Day. Not sure what that means? Onomatopoeia is the term for when the utterance itself is reminiscent of the sound to which the word refers. So on today's four journeys I have heard bark, beep, clap, clash, clucking (at least I think that is the word I heard), fizz, grumbling, peep, pop and puff. I got screeched and smacked in one sentence from a child and its mother. A fly got squished and the kid said 'squish' as he did the murderous deed against the tram window. Someone referred to having tweeted and a dog barked woof and never woofed again the whole journey although it grumbled. National Onomatopoeia Day - obviously!'

Overheard comment: "I started doing some exercise today with a walk in the park. It was much easier than I thought it would be – in fact – it was - a walk in the park! Ha!"

'Today a unicorn got on to the bus without paying. Yes, I know that takes some believing. If I didn't see it with my own eyes I would not have believed it either. It was a young female unicorn about eight years old. The wizard adult that accompanied it on its travels paid the fare for the unicorn. I should be slightly more specific. The unicorn was being ridden in a self-conscious fashion by a beaming girl child who straddled the mythical beast in the most innocent of ways. Not that that took any of its unicorn authenticity away from it, whatsoever. No, not at all. The stark reality was there for all to observe if only they could have looked up from their mobile phones streaming the latest Game Of Thrones episodes. Three stops later the unicorn trotted off with the little girl still clinging on. I tried to take a photo with my mobile phone as they departed the bus but some mythical magic in the air prevented me from doing so.'

Overheard comment: "All the trousers in there were three times too long for me. Maybe I'll grow into them."

'It seems that a new pensioner hobby has sprung to life to be enjoyed whenever they travel on public transport. I have seen them grinning the biggest grin their shiny false teeth will allow, when they think about or practice this enjoyable new game. The new hobby allows them free travel after nine-thirty am and could potentially sharpen their wits and eyesight. "What is it?" you beg of me. It is signage spotting!

To get the best benefit the players should be travelling for around fifty minutes. If they travel with someone a bit hard of hearing they get bonus points for having to repeat themselves. I said "Have to repeat themselves." Here are some good examples of bits of signage I have heard, spoken out loud, recently and the corny OAP comments that invariably follow. By the way, these words have to be spoken with a small amount of drama as if the sign reader has never seen the words before. So with your best loud voice and plenty of pointing at the signs, here we go. For each one you get a point. If your false teeth fall out whilst speaking you lose a point. Inane or corny comments score no points.

"Emergency exit - break with hammer. (that sounds dangerous) Max Headroom. (Wasn't he on the telly?) No entry. (ooer Matron!) Restricted room only. (ooer again Matron!) Smile you are on CCTV. (not with these teeth) Look Both Ways. (how do you do that?) Conduit Close. (I can't see one.) Made To Measure. (that's a Shakespeare play isn't it?) Training

Academy. (is that a school for train drivers?) Self Contained. (that's me) Pay-As-You-Go. (unless you have a free pensioner pass like us) Public and Trade Welcome. (I should think so) A Place of Opportunity. (for what?) Find Your Happy Place. (down the pub) Fighting Animal Testing. (animals shouldn't be forced to do exams) Free Dental Check Up. (get your dentures out Derek) Please Do Not Distract The Driver. (not planning too!) Funky Pots. (what's that all about, painting your own pots?) Brakes On- Relax. (how can you relax with your brakes on?) Paedophiles Crossing (Eh? That can't be right.) Pedestrians crossing!"

'Overheard comment: "Look more grey. It's everywhere. They say grey is the new black. Or is it black is the new grey?"

'You often see personal shopping trolleys heaved onto public transport by sweet old ladies. Their week's groceries, a copy of The Lady and a loaded gun with a hair trigger, are all crushed into a patterned rectangular conveyor on dodgy wheels. It seems more and more clear to me that, contents aside, and that includes the granny gun, what gives their true personalities away is the pattern or design on the trolley. I have seen them with a bold sexy red lips design and wondered (but not for too long) if pensioners have more time on their hands, or any other body parts, for a bit of hot, kiss and don't tell, passion in the bungalow *boudoir*? For anyone who feels inclined to complain about trolleys getting in their way on a bus, it is apposite to remind you that in ye olden days, when granny was a boy, buses were actually called trolley buses. Look that one up if you care too.

Additionally, there are those Anderson wicker models perfect for picnics and a secret depository for spent bottles of Famous Grouse whisky and maybe a even real grouse from the weekend shoot on the council housing estate. And you thought those loud bangs were fireworks. Then there are the two wheeler trolleys with pet animal designs such as unusually coloured poodles, retching cats, hip hop mice showing off their skateboard skills or crazy eyed parrots.

Maybe I exaggerate slightly but there are a middle-aged couple who regularly get on my bus dressed in baggy tee shirts with massive cat face designs and matching cat design trolleys. At home they must have a pair of his and hers wardrobes each spilling over with categorically feline design tee shirts. I say this because every time I see them they have a new pussy cat lovers look to them. It would come as no surprise to me if their whole house wasn't an urban temple to the world of Moggy The Mog with gold litter trays in every room. I bet coach loads of tourist cats arrive every weekend to have a good slope around, leave their scent, nick the resident cats' food and take cat selfies by the famous, swings both ways, Cat Flap of Freedom. In the visitors book the tourist cats can either scratch something positive, spray on a piece of furniture or just take home a few limited edition ceramic replica fleas as souvenirs.

I've seen butterfly trolleys pulled along by their owners who show a wilful ignorance of the so called butterfly effect wherein a very small change in initial conditions (buying an unneeded tube of garlic purée at the supermarket for example) creates a significantly different outcome (less visits from vampire relatives on a Sunday night.)

Some trolleys have logos or slogans on them for all to read and sometimes agree with. Top of this league would be the ones that declare 'I'm Off My Trolley' or 'Pick Me Up, You're About To Pull' and 'This Trolley Is Full Of Sex Aids'. Of course there are the more ironic slogan style trolleys aimed at the frailer members of society who, thankfully, still have their wits left. These may say things like 'Wheels On Fire!', 'This Trolley Contains My Dead Missus', and 'My Other Trolley Is A Porsche.' Lastly, there are the two trolley logos that cause the most consternation in the world of pensioner supermarket shopping – 'Supermarket Security Are All Wankers.' and 'I Love To Purloin Stuff.' I digress, as personally, I am still at the carrier bag stage in life.'

Overheard comment: Thin and frail old lady to a stranger.
"Excuse me lovely but, this morning, were the windows in your house running with compensation?"

'Quite a few people accidentally leave something behind on the bus or tram as they get off. Sometimes they realise their folly as they step on the pavement or platform. They then spin about, quicker than a ballet dancer with head lice, and, panic stricken, rush back to their seat to retrieve their bag, hat or mobile phone. Sometimes the item (if they have remembered it at all) is of so little value that they just leave it on the seat. Such an item might be a newspaper or magazine which can then be recycled/ enjoyed by another passenger. Whether they read it or not depends on their need to soak up any more news of crooked politicians or that ongoing divisive saga called Brexit. Really, we just don't have enough of that kind of journalism.

So imagine my utter delight when a nice magazine was left on the seat opposite me, a magazine I could take home and peruse at leisure. Before you naughtily assume the worst, the front page didn't feature a pouting comely maiden in a state of undress surrounded by bold text hinting at even more salacious pictures in a special four page feature inside. No, this unexpected gift of a magazine was in the form of The People's Friend aimed at any of the older generation who would get excited about wearing incontinence pants whilst going up and down stairs on a Stannah stair lift and urgently crocheting a toy to help The Cat's Protection League.

On my lengthy perusal of The People's Friend magazine I eventually discovered its keywords are comfort, elasticated waist, health and incontinence. Instead of naked twenty-five year old Janet from Bristol on the cover, this magazine has painterly depictions of beauty spots around the British Isles: text that hints of the joyfulness and positivity of the short stories within and topped off with a grisly murder mystery based in the 1930s. Smaller colour photos and text suggest that a vital feature about food safety advice lurks within its hallowed pages and there are brilliant burger recipes to try, as long as your kitchen isn't an unwelcome home to Mr Staphylococcus Listeria and his bio-unfriendly mates. There's a feature on that too.

So, pulling on my trousers with full elasticated waist and gently tapered legs, I eagerly digested articles which told me how to reduce night sweats; informed me that camel's milk is easier on the gut and I got three valuable lessons on easing social anxiety whilst doing the cryptic crossword or sudoku puzzle.

The magazine wasn't without a bit of titillation and I found myself somewhat hot under the collar when I stumbled upon the full page advertisement for 100% Cotton Soft Jersey Nightwear with striking floral motifs. The fifty plus, raven haired temptress modelling the full length night attire was just smoking! I mean she was very attractive not like, you know, smoking in bed. That would be most dangerous but, thinking ahead as a writer, the subject would also make a great safety article for the next issue. Tagline: So hot she set the bed alight!

The People's Friend isn't short on adverts for things the oldies can waste most of their pensions on. On one page alone you could cough up sixty-three quid for 'three fabulous CD box sets all digitally remastered for the best possible sound quality'. To my way of thinking the offer is only worthwhile if you happened to be an ardent fan of The Very Best of American Big Bands, The Greater than Great - Great American Songbook and The Very Best of The Very Best Trad Jazz Ultimate Collection. But, what if you only marginally liked jazz but not riverboat classics. Or that you liked Frank Sinatra, Tony Bennett and Ella Fitzgerald but loathed Doris Day? I know, I know. Who could loathe the adorable Doris Day? But you see my point, I hope.

I flicked the pages ever onward to come across another full page advert (in July, for goodness sake) for three Love, Peace and Joy, collectable Christmas lanterns each featuring a model New England style family home. It was a bit like the ones in the film Home Alone excepting the model houses don't feature an inventive child and two wily but stupid robbers, more is the pity. The model houses, each encased in a lantern, are all part buried in a thick layer of snow and painted to show a golden glow coming from inside. These houses are seen in the daylight so what must their electricity bills be like if they have the lights on all day long? Maybe I am being unkind because the lanterns look like real high quality tat with a price tag to make any right minded purse shake in fear. How much? Only £79.98 plus £9.99 postage. Thank the Lord they all come with a certificate of authenticity! Whatever that means. Who buys this stuff?

The issue I picked up seems to have really gone to town on a two page, recipe packed feature for various lip smacking styles of burger. There are photo illustrated recipes for sweet potato burgers with pesto mayonnaise, an Irish peppercorn studded burger with tricolour coleslaw and sweet potato wedges, and a Quorn ultimate vegan burger (that is piled so ridiculously high with layers that it looks impossible to eat). Just when you think there couldn't be any more, the next page (including what looks suspiciously like pensioner dribble stains on my copy) reveals a barbecue teriyaki burger with chopped spring onions (with an oddly named ingredient of one 'thumb' of ginger - diced finely) and a venison burger with blue cheese and crispy shallots. The only type of burger they don't feature is a burger for people who don't like burgers. Frankly, they can burger off.

Looking at the very bottom of the page is a teaser which promotes tasty breakfast recipes in next week's issue. I am so hungry now from reading about all these burgers that I am going to the newsagent post haste to secure my next week's issue of The People's Friend. Well, I mean, who wouldn't? Hang on, there's more. I told you it was good value.

Stapled in-between a fascinating article celebrating eighty years of The Wizard of Oz and the yellow brick road is a product brochure. But, before we go down that particular route I would like to return to the yellow brick road. This is a road, by the way, that sees phenomenally little in the way of vehicular traffic, if any at all. Thinking about it realistically, anything with a motor ploughing down the yellow brick road at forty miles an hour, or more, would be an instant death sentence for the local Munchkin population, who are dozy beyond belief. Its sole purpose is merely to be a winding path for oddly dressed people, a girl in gingham (who, one day, becomes a gay icon) and a cowardly lion (who doesn't) and a scarecrow who likes to dance. Their deranged mutual hope is in seeing a wizard at the end of it. As if. I think it's about time to check out the contents of this 'must buy' product brochure.

Gosh it seems there is no end of goodies to go credit card crazy on. There's an excellent value ultrasonic pet repellent device, detox foot pads, an assortment of attractive light and flowing kaftans suitable for women and confident men. You can buy value slippers for menfolk who want to shuffle around in the style of an aged granddad with gout, discrete unisex bladder control underwear, and shoes designed for swollen and awkward feet (whatever they are). There's an antibacterial toastie maker that doubles as bath soap on Tuesdays and 250ml spray cans of rust killer with 20% off. Wow! Where did I put my bank card?

It is hard to resist the two white owls on a stand that light up and 'protect' your garden at night. Quite how they are going to do that is anybody's business. No nocturnal thief in their right mind would even think of stealing such a pile of garden ornament crap. Well folks, like myself you may not be tempted to part with any of your money for goods on sale in this product brochure but... and it is a game changer this ... if you spend over £29 you will get a free shopping trolley! Now that is worth considering stocking up on incontinence pants, hanging bird feeders, the three minute oven cleaner and a fluffy microwave omelette maker. But then how many of us own a fluffy microwave?

I guess that's enough sarcastic jollity from me. I am going to settle down now in my brown and grey granddad value slippers, file my nails with my new diamond lustre nail file (now only £3.99), adjust the cat's unisex non slip bra with easy front fastening and read some lovely comforting short stories about love and romance and inbreeding amongst friendly seaside donkeys. Ah, The People's Friend, so glad someone left that on the bus seat for me to enjoy.'

'Now we come to the subject of overhearing about other people's expensive holidays whilst on public transport when (like many) you happen to be in a poor financial position. If you can't afford to live too well and paying bills is a daily problem, then any considerations of anything as crazy frivolous as paying for, and taking a holiday, flies out of the proverbial window. I don't begrudge anyone a short break and even longer holiday, perhaps abroad. These things are part of our pleasures of being alive and I don't have a jealous bone in my body about such matters. It is only when a person broadcasts their ongoing lifestyle as being on an endless succession of exotic and super expensive holidays month after month, year after year, that my smile starts to crinkle at the edges and my eyes become more glazed over than a plate of sticky Chinese spare ribs. People often use the phrase "Don't these people have jobs to go to like most other people? How can they possibly afford it?" How indeed.

"Hey listen up everyone! The wife and I are holidaying in the Seychelles for the third time this year!" they brag. These folk love to show off through pictures and grinning emoticon riddled statements on Facebook and also, in very fine detail, and sometimes a bit too loudly, on public transport. Boorish isn't, by any means, moreish.

One evening, on the Nottingham to Loughborough bus I overheard a man and a woman, at the rear of me, in conversation. It amused me somewhat, despite the fact that I was very skint at the time. He was telling her all about his life, spanning the last ten years travelling the world with his wife. I have recreated the conversation below with a smattering of actual fact and a lot of fun fiction. Believe it or not, he actually started to sound more and more like a travel brochure as well as being terribly privileged and rich. His voice sounded cultured without sounding snobby and her interjections were along the lines of "Oh that's sounds marvellous Gordon! You two are soo lucky! I wish we could afford that! You were there for six months? Gosh how wonderful."

Woman: Hello Gordon! I haven't seen you for years. Where have you been?

Now pause in your reading and go and make a giant mug of tea and stock your plate up with plenty of biscuits and a quality lemon cake. You will need them. You are in for a long haul as they say in the world of trans-Atlantic flights. Fasten your seat belt and enjoy the ride! It may get dippy. "Boarding passes at the ready please."

Man: Yes. My. It must be ten years Sylvia. Time flies. You look pale. You look like you need a holiday, like us. We've practically been all around the world, twice over. Never stopped. We've been to Japan, America, Peru, Australia, New Zealand, Egypt, Greece, Liechtenstein, The Philippines, Greenland, South America, Nova Scotia and up and down the fjords so often we are practically Vikings! You know what? Sometimes I even forget where we were last on holiday, but I do know it wasn't Skegness. Can you believe that? It all blends into one enormous trip. We enjoy it but I guess all that travelling isn't for everybody. And anyway, I mean, who goes to Skegness?

Woman: So where have you been just lately?

Man: We've just been on a Grand Tour of Europe actually. It was a twenty-one days trip originally but we extended it to three months. There is no point going if you are just going for twenty-one days, don't you think? We went by Eurostar, car and plane and took in Paris, Amsterdam, Munich, Bratwurst, Baden Baden, Campania, and we caught every one of the 160 varieties of fish as we explored (by coracle) the Danube delta in Romania. That was interesting. Leaky - but interesting. The wife paddled. She's got stronger wrists than me. Near to Dubrovnik we fought off wild bears with our bare hands, a teaspoon and a sharpened credit card. I think they wanted sex with the wife just because she was wearing a fur coat. Then we went all naturist for a week in the snow capped Carpathian mountains and practised our extreme nude skiing skills. It's a snip at £400 a day.

In Florence we had our pockets picked by rogue street urchin hamsters. Then we went to a place called Mount Zebedee where we met up with Brian and Dougal, a gay farming couple we know. They let us fuss over their cows Ermintrude and Daisy until it was time to go to bed. Sienna was hot, Tuscany was baking, Venice was wet and full of common tourists falling into canals and a strange small person in a red duffel coat who kept disappearing around corners and scuttling over canal bridges. Barcelona was dirty, rowdy and full of Gaudi, We got ill in Seville and roamed around the rugged Roman ruins in Rome. In Paris we got plastered.

Woman: Oh how lovely...

Man: I mean Paris is always very nice. Having been twenty-three times before we are almost like native Parisians. You should see the way I carry my baguette. You have to have it at just the right angle under your arm or the French police fine you. This time though, the wife had French diarrhoea. That's like normal diarrhoea except you can opt for it to be gift wrapped with silvery toilet paper with a *fleur de lis* pattern. Don't laugh. It's true. The local doctor also supplies a big bow to tie around your bottom. It makes you feel so much better as you squat and squirt. Sorry, that's my wife's expression. She can be a little vulgar at times. So that day I explored the Louvre whilst she explored the loo. Another day we spent a lovely afternoon sampling cheese at a high brow specialist cheesemongers. Spent a bloody fortune.

Of course we only eat orgasmic now so the selection was fairly limited. If the wife doesn't actually come whilst she is eating the cheese she spits it out disdainfully. The cheese makers' *Le Pavé* was *parfait*. Have you tasted *Le Pavé? Non?* Oh you should. The goats have worked so hard to produce it and love it when you can stroke their beards. I could spend hours just doing that. My wife had one mouthful of *Le Pavé* and she got so aroused it was like the famous scene from When Harry Met Sally. We paid for the repairs to the table after her fists had smashed a piece off the corner in ecstatic fervour. This time we slummed it and just stayed in a five star hotel, set in its own thirty acres yet close enough to casually sit in nearby cosy and chic boutique cafes and enjoy a coffee and a dizzying selection of gold plated – hand tossed patisserie.

Woman: That sounds expensive.

Man: Not really. You do get a little change out of a hundred euros. It's what we normally pay. Did I tell you about Florence and Tuscany? Stunning landscape. Stunning. Very romantic, if you like that kind of nonsense, and we met the actresses Dame Judy Dench and Helena Bonham – Casserole. They were just lovely. Of course they recognised us straight away. We had supper with them at St Regis. It has gorgeous chandeliers and custom made frescos. If a place doesn't make the effort to provide custom made frescos we avoid it like the plague. Really. You should go there sometime. It's just a simple no fuss four starred *Michelin* restaurant but we didn't want to embarrass Dame Judy and Helena by splitting the bill so we paid for it all ourselves. The bill included the five bottles of wine they had each, and their triple brandies. Between you and me Dame Judy gets a bit greedy with the thousand year old olives stuffed with Basque chillies and hand dusted with rare white truffles. She wolfs them down like sweets from a jar. It's obscene but, you know, she's a dame so what can you do? Helena BC ate her linguine tossed, claws delicately massaged, fussed over within and inch of its life, king lobster with such gluttonous rapidity that most of it ended up in her hair. Not a pretty sight.

Woman: That's really funny. Did you put this on Facebook?

Man: We've stopped with Facebook because it would be a full time job for us putting up all those holiday declarations with Google maps showing that we are at Heathrow soon to be departing the UK for another three month jaunt. It just encourages burglar types breaking into one's abode. We've been luckier than some dear friends of ours – the Ashgrove Hobnobs's – you may know them - they had burglars steal all their priceless Monet's, Piccaso's and an original Art Deco dining set and a treasured packet of milk chocolate digestives. The burglars even had the temerity to make themselves a pot of Imperial Qing Lapsang Souchong tea using our friend's invaluable Yung Cheng period 18th Century porcelain. They broke the handle off the sugar bowl and they never even washed the cups properly. Scum.

Woman: That's not nice.

Man: No it isn't. The least those oiks could have done is wash up properly after themselves. Anyway, my stop is soon. Let me just name drop a bit more because I know you will be utterly fascinated. Michael Palin. There we go. Name duly dropped. By golly. What am I like? We met dear Michael over the Grand Canyon. Literally over the Grand Canyon. By pure coincidence there he was in the next private helicopter flying alongside our own private helicopter. It was so funny. I said to my wife "Look darling – over there – it's our best friend and lovable TV personality - Michael Palin!" We waved to him and he waved frantically in our direction, flashing that affable schoolboy grin of his. It was so nice to see him again. He was on one of his BBC travels no doubt. We couldn't hear what he was saying over the noise of rotor blades. We are always bumping into him in unusual foreign places. One would almost think he was stalking us!

Oh it looks like my stop is coming up soon. I wouldn't normally slum it on the bus with the common garden natives, but I do have to pick up the Jaguar from the little garage owner chappie. We may not see each other for a while because we are planning to go to Iceland to experience the geysers spurting hot liquid like ridiculously randy teenage boys. That's my wife's description incidentally. She can be a little forthright. And so, while we are there we are going to try out some ancient Icelandic ice acupuncture. Apparently, they make you lay down on a cured penguin skin bed, poke you liberally about the person with super thin icicles and leave them in your flesh until they melt completely. They are very strict and if you attempt to get up before the ice has completely melted, they make you listen to hours of Bjork. Imagine that! Then you get a full body massage by an Inuit who uses a pungent oil made up of sea lion sweat, fresh caught herring blood and wild dill that's been soaked in bergamot oil since 1126.

On that note it has been so lovely talking at you. We must do it again in ten years time if we are not on holiday. Oh look, would you believe it there's Angelina Jolie with Bill Gates! Angelina! Bill, old chums! It's me! Fancy you seeing me here! Don't run away. Let me tell you about my holidays.'

Overheard comment: "Did you see in the Sun newspaper about that drunk man and woman who 'performed a sex act' on board the full Manchester to Exeter National Express coach? National Sexpress the Sun called it. Well they would. Apparently, they didn't even know each other before the coach left Manchester! And he was the driver."

'Two old ladies were sat opposite me on the tram this lunchtime each carrying their own copy of the shopping bible, the paper brick like tome known as the Argos catalogue. The two pensioners were dressed in the dowdy loose fitting fashion known as, mental facility escapee. It looked like they were dressed in a pastel coloured sack complimented by baggy stockings. From their look I was led to understand that, back along the tram track, there was a thorny bush complaining how two old farts hair had been dragged through it in a backwards fashion. Quietly revelling in their personal dereliction, these women were thumbing their way through the Argos catalogue on some kind of frantic shopaholic fantasy. As they poured each packed page they would tell the other to check out page so and so and make comments. They occasionally allowed their smudged lipstick shrunken mouths a prurient wheezy giggle and an out of control dribble of joy. Both ladies had chin stubble that Desperate Dan would be proud of. Their random conversation, mostly constructed of reading bits out from the 'You're Good To Go' Argos catalogues went something like this.

"575 Treadmills section. It says to enjoy now and pay six months later. This one's got fourteen speeds with blue tooth connectivity – whatever that is. It's not cheap at £279.99 Doris. I don't think I'll be getting one of them, do you? 579 Exercise

81

bike with variable tennis control. I've read that wrong. Tension control. Batteries required.

Credit card representative 29.9% APR variable. No thanks. My neighbour had one of them credit cards. Got herself in a lot of debt. She's been dead ten years and she's still paying it off now from beyond the grave.

597 Look at him on his dual resistant rower – the ultimate cardio dracula exercise. £599.99. I might get myself a toy boy like that. Shall I get you one?" They break off to giggle and drool, adjust their faded Paisley pattern nightgowns at the crotch level, then start up again.

"Argos do all sorts of lights you know. It says here they've got a great selection of easy fit shades and there's one with hares on it. Not like hairs from your head – like a big rabbit. Page 199. You can have shades of 'glam to glitz up your home' and you can buy this here glass chandelier for £100. That'd look nice in the downstairs toilet at the home. I like smelly candles. There's few in here look and diffusers – whatever they are. I used to light up a smelly candle after me hubby used to fart. We got through no end of them Yankee candles.

Look here. This is ridiculous. There's page after page of kiddies toys. We never had anything like that did we Beryl? In our family we had to make do and play with an old beer crate from the Off Licence and juggle with a pair of second hand mouldy oranges wrapped up in pages from The Sporting

Chronicle. It taught us to be creative. Kids are spoilt these days. They don't appreciate it.

Have you seen the amount of health and beauty products there is in this catalogue? Make up and the like. When I were a teenager, and that's a long time ago I can tell you, I was told I was a natural beauty – no make up required. Well, we couldn't afford make up in them days anyway. I used to scrub me self with half a tin of stale baked beans balanced on a slice of burnt toast. It would bring me skin up lovely. Then I'd splash myself liberally from a bottle of malt vinegar and the the boys would come running for miles around. Oh look it's our stop coming up. Don't forget your catalogue dear."

'Sometimes the odder end of fellow travellers try any trick in the book to get your attention even though they don't know you and somehow it becomes very necessary to quickly think up ways to escape their presence. Even though I have never actually come across this alleged book of tricks in a bookshop or online I did encounter a very tricky traveller the other day on an early morning trip to work, on the tram.

There weren't that many people on this particular tram. At a stop just outside the city centre a very large man in a wheelchair rolled into a space for wheelchairs just opposite me. He looked a bit rough around the edges, an older tough guy type straight from central casting. His pitted and pockmarked face bore a few scars and his short haircut gave the impression he'd done it himself with a pair of blunt garden shears whilst wearing a blindfold and tortuously tickled by mad monkeys high on beetle nuts.

As he sat in his wheelchair it came slowly to my attention that his left leg finished rather abruptly at his knee. The knot on the knee of his grubby grey trousers gave that away, as did the lack of lower limb. Once the tram doors had closed the tram set off again. The guy looked at me. No that's wrong. The guy stared at me. Nope that's wrong too. The guy glared at me in the same threatening manner as a half crazed dragon who'd had his morning sleep disturbed and someone had dared to come into his lair to steal his golden hoard. Close enough.

"Alright?" he asked. I nodded and murmured something along the lines of "Yes thanks." which had "Mummy the nasty weird man is talking to me. Make him go away!" as a silently fearful subtext clinging on nervously to its edges. I sipped my Costa coffee and tried not to look at him.

"Nice coffee?" he growled. "Uh uh." said I, in return. Then I am sure the guy's eyes went blood red as he came out with an unexpected torrent of completely random questions whilst thumping his half leg violently with his beefy fist. "What's my pin number? Who won the lottery? I said, who won the lottery? Do you like bombs? Why doesn't the sky fall down? Tell me the number of your house. My house is on fire. Is your house on fire? Do you like cabbage? Do you know Dr Bonkers? Does he know my pin number? Want to see my gun, do you? Have you got an iPhone? What's your phone number? Does it begin with seven? I can get the answer out of you. They all begin with seven don't they? Is that a conspiracy? Do you want to see me when I am really angry? I can breathe fire like a dragon. Can you? What do you think about brown sauce? Where are you on Lord of The Rings? I want to touch your ring Gollum."

Suddenly, I noticed an invisible friend trying desperately to get my attention at the other end of the tram. So I gingerly got up and walked past the crazy wheelchair guy to sit with Harvey my invisible rabbit friend and a few other passengers. As I sat down in the safety of Harvey's company I could still hear him firing questions at my now vacant seat in front of him. A few days later I saw this man on the tram again randomly questioning a well dressed man with a smart beard and the poor victim had same unnerved look in his eyes I must have had. Thankfully I have never seen the crazy guy in the wheelchair since. Maybe the sky fell down over him. And he never did get my phone number.'

Overheard comment: Middle-aged woman to her friend. "So we're going out for a meal Monday, then we're going out for a meal Tuesday. Wednesday we're been taken out for an Indian meal. Thursday we're staying in. Then on Friday we're going out for a pub meal. We might go out for another meal at the garden centre at the weekend."

'This evening on the bus into town there is an old man seated behind me who keeps bursting out into song. He isn't subtle about it and seems to have a preference for English folk songs. We all have no choice but to hear the lyrics tell us 'My father was a Spanish merchant...' and something about 'plucking flowers all wet with dew' and asking if the lady would be offended 'if I walk and talk with you.' There were a few verses and the jolly chorus of 'Oh no, John, no John, no John no!' The old chap really seemed to revel in the suggestive verse 'On her bosom are bunches of posies, On her breast where flowers grow. If I should chance to touch that posy she must answer yes or no.' The words bosom and breast get a specially bawdy vocal expression. The word posy sounds suspiciously like pussy coming from him. Maybe he has a cat. I half expect that he expects the other passengers all to join in with the 'Oh no John...' chorus. If only life were that simple.'

'Quite often, on bus travel, the bus can get delayed by passengers dithering about sorting out their exact change to pay for their fare. Why they couldn't have done that at home or whilst in the queue for their eventual bus arrival, goodness knows. Students can be the worst at this. You also get groups of passengers who very rarely travel on buses but, decide to 'slum it' to get from their home to the railway station or airport link cheaply on a bus, with the commoners, rather than take a taxi. All the holidaying family pile on with their multiple suitcases and haven't given any thought, not only how to pay their fare when the bus company doesn't give change, nor the fact that their ten minute discussion with the driver is delaying the service for those that have to be at work. When some of them get around to getting the correct change all sorted out they are so flustered by the event and the metaphorical daggers being thrown at them by the other passengers that they then drop all their coins all over the floor of the bus which invariably roll outside, and into the gutter. The whole set of the, now very annoyed passengers, who are just keen to get on with their journey, do a collective face palm and a record-breaking group sigh.'

Overheard comment: Man "Yes, honest to God I am absolutely one hundred thousand percent sure. Definitely. I think."

'At times you get the cocky young kids who just won't sit down on the bus or tram even though their parent has told them to so many shrill times. Even as an adult you get bored with hearing the same refrain over and over. "SIT down, NOW. If you don't sit down you are going to be in so much trouble with your Dad (whoever he is) when we get home. SIT DOWN NOW! I said SIT down. Look the bus is leaving. If you FALL OVER I'm not going to be to blame."

The demands become less like telling a naughty child what to do and more like giving a deaf mongrel commands. "Sit! I said sit. Sit. SIT. SIT down NOW. You are embarrassing me. Stop giggling. It's not funny. FINE you fall down and see where that will get you. No, I'm not going to pick you up. SIT. NOW. I am not telling you again. Everybody is looking at you. SIT DOWN. Look, you nearly fell over then. Sit next to your sister. She's a good girl. Stop hitting her. We are getting off in a minute so just sit down. Next to that master then. Right I've bloody had enough. We are getting off at the next stop. Ring the bell. It's up there. Ring the bell or the bus driver man will go straight past. RING IT! Thank you. Come on. We are getting off and YOU are straight to bed with no supper. Why are you sitting down? We are getting off. Stand up. I said STAND UP! Will you, for once, do as you are told!"

Overheard comment: Actually, this one was just an enormously irritating constant "So ..." at the beginning of each and every sentence a young woman uttered in a dull as swamp water conversation with her phone friend. "So... what did you do last night? So... we went to Yates' Lodge except it was closed, wasn't it. So... then we went to Spoons. So... he's a real tight arse. So... I ended up paying for everything. So... when we come out (she meant *came* out) I got in a taxi quick like so he was left to get home on bus or whatever. So... we're not speaking now. So... it's dead quiet in the house. So... what did you get up to? What? You are joking me! Needlework? So... so you've starting sewing have you? So sewing ..."

'There is a mental health condition called misophonia in which negative emotions, thoughts and even physical conditions are triggered by certain types of noise and behaviour and it drives the sufferer crazy. It is sparked off by other people chewing loudly with their mouth open. This happens a lot on public transport and I think I suffer mildly from this to the point where I have even moved seat when possible to escape the sloppy and rampant masticating noises replicating an over-busy dustbin wagon on heat. It does make me terribly tense.

Similarly, but probably not covered by the same medical term, is when empty plastic bottles or empty cans roll around the floor of the public transport I am travelling on. Nobody bloody picks them up! Nobody. Surely other people find these fancy free empty drinks containers clattering and rolling from pillar to post, cheekily cavorting from under a seat to the bus door and back, bothersome. They do, don't they? Surely.

Sometimes they still have an element of liquid in them which sloshes out as the drink container crashes up against a bag or a pair of shoes. Then the floor is all sticky and still no-one bothers to reach down and pick up the bottle or can. I got on a bus midday yesterday and saw one of these delinquent plastic Coca Cola bottles grinning under a seat like it was just waiting for the bus to start up to start rocking and rolling like a sexed up 1950s teenager. For once, I reached down and picked the gummy bottle up and placed it in the bin. "There!" I said to a young stranger seated near me. "That won't be annoying anyone today, will it?!" I felt quite proud like I had done a public duty. She looked slightly abashed and said "Thank you. It was mine. I couldn't be bothered to go all the way to the bin." I rest my case – in a puddle of sticky Coca-Cola.'

Overheard comment. On tram. "I wish they'd shut up with that tannoy. We all know where we're going, don't we? And it's not even in a Nottingham accent is it?"

'It's one of those days when it seems that all the vocally annoying people in the world have got on my bus at once. Note I say 'my bus'. I would equally love to describe it as 'my ultimate haven of peace on wheels' but alas, National Calm Day is not happening today or any day soon. In one single, twenty minute, journey we have the child with a voice so piercing you'd think he'd swallowed a dog's squeaky toy on purpose. It's joined by more small children who have absolutely no volume control at all. Every one of these angelic bellowing sweethearts continues to 'entertain' myself and my fellow beleaguered travellers with their small gobby personalities still locked in - wild abandoned kids at the crèche - mode. Their mothers are too busy gassing on their mobiles to ask the kids to keep quiet. I must invest in some industrial earplugs.

There's another noisy bleeder at the back of the bus watching a film that has to be turned up full volume so that all the other passengers can enjoy all the shouting, screaming and madcap car chase effects while the world is blown to smithereens by evil bad boy aliens who are accompanied on their destructive course by smaller screaming toddler aliens. Or so it would seem. I must add Screaming Toddler Aliens – the movie to my bucket list of things to watch before I pop my clogs.

Oh great, a regular well known idiot is now boarding my bus. Currently, we have the dubious pleasure of Trevor (he has a name badge) the lanky whistling Asda supermarket worker who has finished his shift. Trevor swans around like he is an apprentice fashion model. Launching himself up the stairs, three at a time, the grinning moron plonks himself down on a top deck seat where he continues relentlessly with his bothersome tuneless whistle that he has been practising all day long in the Asda fruit and veg section. Now it is time for him to generously share his depressing whistles with the top deck crowd. Oh joy of joys. My fervent prayers for the bus to unexpectedly stop and rather violently knock him out is not granted by the public transport gods today. I have been praying so hard using a combination of visualisation techniques and Pound Shop voodoo dolls.

Closer to me, some man on his mobile decides to get in touch with the whole of his endless contact list in order to obstreperously discuss with, each and every one of them, how much simpler life was before mobiles. He obviously isn't speaking loudly enough today because he has to keep asking, full volume, "Can you hear me okay?" On the twentieth time of asking him asking if he is audible enough I want to shout "Yes mate, we CAN bloody hear you, unfortunately!" My once bountiful supply of mental throwing daggers is rapidly running out.

Later on, just as all the nerve-wreckers have all got off and I assume peace has, at last, descended all around little old sensitive me, a rogue mobile games player right behind me pumps up the volume on his ear blasting crescendo of battle effects and obligatory screaming. I have had enough. I reach quietly into my bag, lift out the object I need, twist on the silencer and, with one bullet, obliterate the bastard iPlayer and shoot its owner stone dead. A shocked hush lingers for a second amongst my fellow passengers and as the gossamer grey gun smoke clears I get a grateful round of applause for my vigilante deed. I get off the bus whistling my best cowboy hero tune, tunelessly.'

Overheard comment: "There was somebody flossing their teeth next to me on this tram yesterday. Flossing their teeth! On the tram! I ask you. Honestly, I didn't know where to look! I thought people clipping their nails was bad enough! Whatever is next!? Inserting a tampon?"

'The discussions around the *joys* of travelling on public transport often begin with a common opening question. I wonder if you can guess what that is? I will elucidate. The question is "Why is it that..?" This universal question is usually followed by some minor atrocity or uncomfortable feeling regarding the public behaviour of others in common situations. The atrocity that gets the biggest attention is when a human's personal space has somehow been violated. This can be the story of the creepy stranger who chooses to sit next to you even though there are plenty of seats available for them to sit their weirdness on, or other, less fraught variations.

The intrusion can move from "Is it a good book?" which can be particularly freaky if you are not actually reading at the time. Otherwise this odd enquiry can open up a whole Open University's worth of discussion of what merits the idea of 'good' in a book.

According to social scientists our personal spaces are measured out as public (fairly distant), social (acceptable and relatively easy to escape), and intimate (you really know the person in your space well i.e. intimately). This may include actual kissing or, in a lengthier, less attractive description, happily swapping friendly warm germ spittle. Other qualifying comparative translations exist. For now we will go with kissing or snogging or vigorous tongue lashing.

Some social media guidelines on how to deal with those unwanted space invaders (no guys not the 1978 arcade game invented by Tomohiro Nishikado) are a bit random and unreal. For example I found this on the internet. I might have made a few things up.

What to do if someone is invading your space:

1. Accept it.
2. Lean away from the person or take a step back so he or she will take the hint.
3. Come right out and say you are uncomfortable with being so close.
4. Give them lots of money to go away.
5. Regale with them stories of your pets and how you lost a guinea pig at the age of six and have never fully recovered. Warn of unexpected fitting attacks.
6. Give them the phone number of an enemy and pretend it is your private number.
7. Threaten to be sick, with a degree of urgency, on their new shoes. Then do it.
8. Explain broadly, and with the aid of a baseball bat, why it is that you need more space.

If it were me I would like to imagine myself brave enough to say "Oh hi! You there – you very heavy, damp and sweaty person. I feel that your act of virtually sitting my lap today, and bear in mind I have no clue who you are buddy, is bordering on us getting a tad over familiar. I seriously hope you agree. I don't care a toss if the bus/tram/train/gondola is full. I object to you stroking my thigh like it is a long lost pet. Your underarm odour, although I am holding my breath like a deep sea diver with a death wish, frankly stinks like a freshly unearthed corpse. Please don't cry. Increased wetness won't help this situation whatsoever. They say that crowding often isn't intentional and that kindness and humour can often diffuse a situation but right now I am not asking you, but outright demanding, that you shift your lardy ass as far away as you can from my distraught and insanely squashed personage. I know my sentences are bit long but I like to be expressive. Frankly mate you have legs like giant hams and I would helpfully suggest that you would be more at home being dry cured and suspended upside down in the window of a Spanish charcuterie. No offence." So to use that phrase we opened with. 'Why is it that... they would never listen to all those words you have just uttered in protest and still feel the need to squash you into the window frame as if nothing is untoward?'

Overheard comment: Woman "Well you know what an imposter he is – stealing her boyfriend from right under her nose."

'Some days you just feel in the mood for improving your lapsed French or German language skills whilst travelling by early morning public transport, don't you? You don't? Oh I thought everyone did that. I really did. So much so, that nobody would be in the slightest sense put out if I started naming things I see around me in French or German, accidentally out loud. What about singing full volume in

French in public instead of just in my head? Is that frowned upon too? *Ooh la la!* Well luckily for my fellow travellers I never did do the singing bit. I have often named things in a foreign tongue just for fun to see what I could remember. You know, basic stuff like dog, cat, tree, bus, tram, seat, passenger, house, prostitute, drug dealer, armed police. That sort of everyday stuff. So imagine me sat on a crowded bus or tram gazing around and part thinking in another language. *Allons y!* Bring out your street furniture and body parts and let's call them by another name!

Le mamelon (nipple – glimpsed on cold days) *le cou* (neck – seductive on hot days) *l' épaule* (shoulder – handy for crying on and hanging bags on) *la fesse* (bum) *l' aisselle* (armpit - best stayed away from on public transport) *la téte* (head) *le coude* (elbow – useful for nudging people out of the way when getting off the bus) *la gorge* (throat – handy for sliding a knife across in a frantic *noir* travelling murder fantasy) and *l'épiglotte* (epiglottis). It is amazing how often the word for epiglottis comes up in general French chit chat. I can't think of many actual examples right now except maybe "*Pardonez moi, j'ai faime. Ou est le café l'épiglotte?*"

Then I check out all the different types of human there are around me. We have *le bébé* (baby) *l' enfant* (child – but sometimes mistaken for elephant especially if they are especially chubby) *le garçon* (boy or waiter or boy waiter) *la fille* (girl) *l'adolescente* (awkward spotty person between 13 – 19) *l'adulte* (anybody above 19 years old) *le homme* (bloke or name of a French men's magazine with free samples of after shave and far too many glossy adverts and ridiculously attractive and unavailable French men who are smoking in one definition or other) *la femme* (woman or woman's magazine with free samples of perfume and far too many glossy adverts and ridiculously attractive and unavailable French women who are smoking in one definition or other).

En route we may spy *l'autoroute* (motorway) *les signalisations* (road markings) and a foreign word that, weirdly, the English spell checker didn't think was wrong. Then we get to words which, frankly are a bit of a mouthful like *le parking réservé personnes handicapées* (disabled parking) *le passage clouté* (pedestrian crossing or an archaic but polite expression for constipation i.e. *mon passage est un peut clouté*) *l' embouteillage* (traffic jam – sometimes expressed as *l' embouteillage marmalade* when oranges are more available).You don't want to be exceeding *la limitation de vitesse* (speed limit – meaning anything over eighty miles an hour on the *Champs-Éllysées* or fifty mile per hour down a ridiculously narrow, parked up, back street in Marseilles at night. *La circulation* (moving traffic and nothing to do with blood in your veins).

Over to German, a language that likes to add wordsstucktogetherinordertomakeoneword. But, *Gott Sei Dank*, (thank the Lord) not always. The benefit of writing in German is that there are less accents to waste time with and some are delightfully short and to the point. This means that we don't lose valuable beer drinking and bratwurst and pretzel eating time.

On the roads the Germans enjoy words like *der Busfahrer* (bus driver) *der Taxifahrer* (taxi driver) *der Lastwagenfahrer* (lorry driver) *der Verkehr* (the transport) *Parkuhr* (parking meter) *das Geldbuße* (parking fine) *Einbahn* (one way) *die Überholspur* (outside lane) *der Verkehrspolizist* (traffic policeman) *die Geschwindigkeitsbegrenzung* (speed limit) *die Geschwindigkeitsüberschreitung bekommen* (to get a speeding fine) *vor Gericht erscheinen* (to appear in court) *Richterspruch* (Judge's decision) *schändlich* (shameful) i*m Gefängnis sein* (to be in prison).

On a similar language based theme I love hearing people speaking their own languages as I travel about. I find it one of the genuine joys of travelling on public transport. Sometimes there are so many foreign languages on the go at once, if I close my eyes, I feel like I am on holiday.'

'Travelling to my work place at the supermarket on a Sunday morning is often a quiet affair as few people work on a Sunday, except those in modern day retail, public transport employees and the homewards bound, still drunk or comatose, Saturday night revellers. I would try to organise the timing of my journey so that I had time to go to a nice coffee shop, like Caffè Nero or Costa Coffee, for a pre-work chill out to enjoy a cappuccino and a yummy almond croissant. This was a bit of relaxed leisure before reluctantly starting my job on the meat and fish counter at nine-thirty.

It was something to look forward to each week; a good time where I could relax with the rest of the world at leisure. However, it wasn't always peace and quiet when the café door burst open and several young mums bustled through with their child buggies and attendant kiddies and all their lovely pandemonium. I started to make it a point not to sit anywhere near the coffee shop door for fear of being bashed into. The draft from the open door could be quite chilly, even in the summer. I didn't want to get run over by any rogue buggy and pesky child combo suddenly let loose and thus destroy this old guy's Sunday tranquillity. The mums would be in full clamorous 'let's talk about our darling kids' mode and there'd be everlasting, adult to children, discussions over what the children would like to eat and drink.

This made me bring out my finest ironic smile (I have a selection to chose from) because when I was a child, in the 1950s and 1960s, I had no possibility of choice in what I was going to eat. I just had to eat and drink what I was given, albeit my café food was often in the pleasing shape of a chip cob with greedy amounts of tomato sauce glugged out of a large plastic tomato. At home my old fashioned parents might have said to me, in a kindly fashion, "What do you fancy to eat? Shall we have fish fingers with our mashed potatoes and peas?" You should be aware this question wasn't one that offered choice. It was a simple declaration of fact disguised as an enquiry. No answer was needed. Fish fingers, mashed potatoes and peas was, point blank, what we were all getting for tea. This topic has been a regular and amusing chatting point when I have spoken to different generations of parents on the bus and tram.

Back in the café one Sunday, a particular childhood memory came flooding back to me when I noticed that a clumsy child was spilling its milkshake all down its front. Please realise that I am not the biggest fan of children with food and drink all over their faces. Not being a parent myself, this messy vision doesn't have the cute appeal it does to some doting parents and creators of photographic greetings cards. Ice cream, for example, should go into the mouth and eaten, not smeared all around the mouth and half way up a little imp's snotty nose. Bless 'em all.

When I was around eleven years old I had been taken to the dentist one morning to have my very first filling done. My mouth was still numb when my mum took me to a working class café in a small arcade in Derby to have a nice milkshake for being a brave boy at the dentist. The much anticipated strawberry milkshake was brought to our chequered table top complete with striped plastic straw. I loved strawberry milkshakes as much as any child. Popping the straw into the right hand side of my, still very numb but eager mouth, I sucked at the thick fruity and milky liquid. Instead of residing in my mouth for few delightful moments and slipping happily down my throat, the cold milkshake just poured out the other side and all down my shirt front. The shirt, like the memory, was ruined. Fifty odd years later I still recall this incident whenever I encounter milkshakes and have hated going to the dentist ever since.'

Overheard comment: Woman to young boy. "Walk straight and stop dragging your heels Achilles!

'One of the two bus services I can take from my village to Nottingham goes a circuitous route through a big housing estate on a hill. At the top of the hill and rather conveniently close to the graveyard, is an old folks home. Some of the caring staff at this home for the elderly are middle aged black ladies from Nigeria and the Caribbean. On a Sunday morning the bus service is limited to once an hour and therefore to miss your bus anywhere remote, like the old folks home, means a wait of another hour before the next service passes. There are usually three of these lady carers who presumably finish their shift at eight o'clock in the morning. And most Sundays it feels like they are all living in an alternative, indolent – let's just take it easy now girls – Caribbean time.

The thing that jolts them out of their dreamy reverie is the sudden and solid apparition of the double decker number ten bus arriving. Luckily for them the old folks home stop is also a bus timing stop. Like a rare scene cut from the film Groundhog Day, each Sunday sees two of the three blue uniformed women running hell for leather to get the bus. Behind them is either Bridget, Lilian or Akosua and those in the lead are shouting and laughing to the one lagging behind to hurry up or miss the bus.

They all bundle on to the vehicle with massive smiles as they fish out their passes or small change. Then they head for the back of the bus where they pass the time of the journey joking and talking at volume but with such jocularity that I often feel that I am a grumpy old white git in comparison. I look forward to this stop on the journey just so I can experience these three rays of sunshine for twenty minutes.'

Overheard comment: "Have you got some tissues? I think I am going to have a bad nosebleed from my head."

'This rather windy morning my bus to town is shaking about more than normal. There is also a funny grunting noise coming from either, a bus pass carrying warthog, or the red-faced man in the seat behind me. He sounds like one who suffers badly from constipation. The grunting noise is getting rhythmical along with the swaying of the bus. Just now a different interpretation has ejaculated into my mind. I sincerely hope that the noise he is making isn't a precursor to him having a rather too realistic sexual fantasy on the bus. Sometimes I wish I could drive.'

Overheard comment: "I call this half-nine bus, the pensioner express. I've never seen so many people grinning. Look there's dozens of 'em getting on. All carpet slippers, polished dentures and free bus passes."

'It's late November. The sky is still forebodingly dark as we leave the city towards Beeston. I should have remembered to bring my washboard and snare brush with me because between myself (on washboard) and the bubble gum blower, the shoe shuffler, the loud violent cougher, the young bloke with the twitchy leg and the genteel lady sneezer we could get a cool

101

Blues rhythm section going on this morning's bus. I do feel a song coming on. All together now!'

Overheard comment: "What's it called? You can go on this thing where you do things and then it comes up with the answer."

'A dozen Japanese schoolgirls; older teenagers in short skirts, have just got on my bus. Every one of them is wearing one of those face masks like surgeons wear – but made out of pink and black silk. Either our English atmosphere is hiding something deadly us British cannot see or smell, and we are all doomed to gasp out our last before this bus journey ends, or some beastly bounder outside has farted the worst fart in the world. A third option is that we are all going to be kidnapped by a bunch of odd but attractive oriental girls dressed up to tantalise and tie up the menfolk. Number three has always been my lucky number.'

Overheard comment: Two older ladies talking about a play one of them has just seen.

First lady. "It was translated from the original Norwegian but there was lots of bad swearing in this modern version. I'm pretty sure that Ibsen didn't keep saying 'fuck' every ten minutes in his day."

Second lady. "I bet he did. But maybe it was more like 'fjork'."

'Talk about co-incidence. This one is like freaky Wednesday man! Right across the outside top area of this double decker bus is a big family portrait of the cast of The Addams Family – The Musical Comedy along with enormous gothic gold lettering of the title. The Addams Family musical is coming to Nottingham. So that's on the outside. Imagine my surprise to find myself followed onto the bus by a replica Addams Family except that they seem to have absolutely no awareness that they bear any likeness to the real Addams Family. It is truly uncanny. My mouth opens in disbelief as they all file on, one kooky personality after another. There's Morticia, Gomez, Lurch, Pugsley, Uncle Fester, Grandma and Wednesday. Pugsley even has a pudding bowl haircut, a very gormless thick set look and a striped tee shirt! You could not make it up! I swear I am about to hear the bouncy theme tune and finger clicking any second now. Immediately I am starting to giggle and my creativity goes into overdrive as I imagine that the change for their 'family ticket' bus fares is being handed over by the dis-embodied hand known as Thing.'

Overheard comment. One teenage boy to his cronies on the back seats of the top deck of the bus. "The narky bus driver is the same one we got that time we all got off and then we mooned him. Let's do it to him again. Go on. It'll be a right laugh!"

'This might be an older person thing or my, largely tolerant, inner grammar moderator speaking but, have you ever sat listening to fellow passengers whose pronunciation and grammatical use of regular words is so bad that you find yourself correcting them in your thoughts? You do too? Phew, I like fort it were just me innit.

Depending on my mood, another person saying "Should of..." instead of "Should have..." can either make my eyebrows momentarily raise in Roger Moore style amusement or steam start to come out of my grammar offended ears. I know this is sad but I often find myself mentally correcting words like when for instance is said as *frinstance*. It's hard to ignore the word ignore when a person constantly says *eggnore*. It brings out the deranged Wildebeest in me when going to is articulated as *gnu or gunnoo*. It is hardly effective use of the English language when effects, as in 'sound effects', turns into *affects* and effected becomes *affected*.

Just so you know, something looks amazing not *looks amaze*. "Look a maze" - is the sort of thing a person might say when confronted by a high hedged network of paths through which one has to find a way. I've even seen that mistake on a food poster at the Nottingham railway station. 'Eat more amaze' it read. Short of shouting like a loon, "Eat more amazingly! Not - eat more amaze!" at a poster at six o'clock in the morning, surrounded by barely awake commuters, I carried that error in my head all the way to work. It sat there all day niggling me until I had to go back to the poster on the way home to see if a marketing bod had realised their error and corrected it. Funnily enough, they hadn't.

To continue: Immaculate has an I at the front and is not pronounced *macculate*. Just don't or *dunna* get me started (oh you have) on the following clumsy contractions for isn't it, *intit,* couldn't it *cuntit,* wouldn't it *wuntit,* shouldn't it *shuntit,* and doesn't it *duntit.* There are even Latin based mistakes made when people say vice versa as vice(a) versa. Or, (laughs like a drain) is that the other way round?

Then I hear the types of shortcut sentences completely missing out words like *a, an* and *the* and even (grammar term alert) prepositions like *to.* For example "I'm going shops. Are you coming shops?" "Have you been pub?" "Give us money." "She went park with baby and had nom noms." "He gorron tram without ticket."

It's not just me you know. Some friends who own a local ironmongers shop say that some customers ask for refuge bags instead of refuse bags. The local butcher said he has heard people say autumn(on)al for autumnal and has lost count of hearing parents say to their children "When you are all growed up." as opposed to all grown up. Before I go grammar cop crazy I will end this piece by saying that, even months later, I am still shaking my head at 'Eat more amaze.'

'Say the words brief encounter and a lot of people would think Brief Encounter the famous 1945 dramatic and romantic film directed by David Lean. It starred Celia Johnson and Trevor Howard as the tentative lovers Laura and Alec who meet at a train station. Their lives are forever changed by this unexpected brief encounter. Well, that is an awfully nice British story of pleasant intelligent people who think they are falling in love.

My personal brief encounter, that I am about elaborate upon, isn't in any way romantic. Not at all.

I privately grew to call him Mr Potato Head and first briefly encountered him early one very wet morning at the bus shelter in the village. Because it was raining I moved aside to let him under the shelter. This token gesture of politeness was taken as an open opportunity for Mr Potato Head to talk *at* me. It didn't take me too long to quickly realise that the man was an unsettling bore. He became one of those people who ask you a question then proceed to talk over your truncated answer with their own un-relatable tiresome subjects which fully embrace the minutiae of their work, their work colleagues, and the hated boss man known as the gaffer. Mr Potato Head's drone could give the world's strongest sleeping tablets, meant to sedate pumped up race horses, a total run for their money.

I'll give you an idea of how brain numbingly dull his mono-tonal, virtually one sided, discourses could be. He worked in a some kind of cardboard packing factory and when he spoke ancient trees would give up life and turn themselves to dust to escape his draining and dreary tones. Thinking back, he was like a bus stop vampire in brown overalls. When you read Mr Potato Head's ramble below bear in mind this was the first time he had ever met me.

Mr Potato Head: "They're all trying to get me into trouble. They're saying that I haven't been doing me job properly in plant. It's rubbish! It's them that are cutting corners. Some on 'em have told gaffer and gaffer has 'ad me in his office like. Do you know Folders Packing Company? It's on the other side of town. What we do is – there is your four sided carton, two foot by three, with two flaps either side before it's been put together. I take the two flaps and fold 'em inwards this a way and that a way. You listening? That there carton then gets foam put into it by a machine called a Brit- Foamster 36XB. It's a full capacity flexi-foam constructor that grafts 24/7 making foam pellets.

You listening son? It's important this. If that bit of the job goes down, then the whole plant goes down and we have to stop work. Don't want gaffer getting on at me again for summat like that. So, the strappin' goes on this a way and that a way. It's not like military strapping that some companies use. That's dead expensive so we use a cheaper one which sometimes, not always, but sometimes, comes unstuck and we have to do it all again. God only knows 'ow much that would all cost if we packed it, sealed it and shipped it all the bloody way out to Norway, Nairobi or Lithuania or where have you, and they weren't happy 'n sent it all back again. You get me? Heaven help us if they're the wrong size. You listening? You look half asleep. I'm not wasting my breath here am I mate? Where was I?"

Me: "Cardboard?"

Mr Potato Head: "As I said, they have to be exactly the right size otherwise they get sent back and the gaffer gets it in the neck. Then we all get it in the neck. But I'm not allowed to go on about it. "Crack on Spud" they tell me "or you're out." Let me tell you now son. We can't be a mill of a thou out. Do you know what that means? One mill of a thousand! You are talking 2.5 of an agronomic temperature gauged triple swivel flange European fitting that's used to extricate the chimping system. 2.5. You can't imagine can you mate? Two point bleeding five tapping away non-stop at the chimper... blah blah blah. You listening mate?"

Me: "Not really. You lost me at plant."

Mr Potato Head (Spud) caught me at the same bus stop every day for several days after this first brief encounter and he told me the exact same story every time with the same worryingly blank stare in his eyes. If I saw him on the way to, or actually standing at the bus shelter, I would leg it to another stop to avoid him. I am pleased to say that unlike Celia Johnson's character Laura I never had a piece of smut in my eye for him to wipe away with the damp end of his presumably grubby handkerchief embroidered with his initials M.P.H.'

Overheard comment: "I've got a husband at home but he doesn't talk. All he does is eat, sleep and fart. I'd get more conversation out of a dead dog."

'Four young men got on my bus with a single large pizza each. I assumed they got them at Asda as we arrived at the stop by the supermarket in an area called West Bridgford, south of the city of Nottingham. At first I thought they were carrying cooked pizza and were going to stink the bus out by wolfing down their American Sizzler, Cheese Meltdown, Veggie

Supreme, Pepperoni/Meat Feast or the sickly sounding BBQ Steak and Cheese. On closer inspection I see that the pizzas are cold and wrapped in cling film. Then I notice that these quiet young men are all holding their pizzas out in front of them, like a waiter would a tray of drinks, rather than down by their side hidden, perhaps inside a carrier bag. They don't call me hawk eyes for nothing.

Maybe they weren't going to eat them at all. Maybe this way of transporting the pizza was some 'Create Your Own' performance art event in which the young men, their stone cold - stone baked pizzas and the bus passengers reactions were secretly being documented and filmed. Maybe we would all receive invites to a major arts award as artistic collaborators. Maybe we'll never know because the youngsters have just filed off the bus two stops later with their pizzas held out in front of them at the same angle. Life, and art can be a mystery sometimes.'

'On a late evening bus journey I overheard something mantra like muttered through gritted teeth by a middle-aged man to his travelling companion about a woman on the front seat nearest the bus driver. The woman was talking loudly and very much non- stop to the driver for fifteen minutes as he navigated his route in the dark.

The talkative woman kept repeating "Really! Oh wow!" or "Yeah yeah yeah!" to whatever the driver was saying. There was a distinct sense that the other passengers were getting fed up with hearing her as she shouldn't be talking to the driver while he was in transit.

"Shut up. Shut up. Shut the... Shut up talking." muttered the man quietly, whilst slowly shaking his head in frustration. "I'm going to have to say something in a minute. I am. There she goes again. "Oh really oh wow." She's really getting on my nerves. Shut up. Right one more time. One more time and that's it. You aren't allowed to talk to driver are you? It does say so up front. I'm definitely going to... oh here's our stop."

All three of them got off at the same stop and I saw them engage in polite late-evening conversation as the bus left the stop and they disappeared into the night. I expect you are thinking "Oh really? Oh wow!" and I say "Yeah yeah yeah. It's true."

Overheard Comment: "It drives me mad. I need to get my car back. These buses are just full of sniffers, snorters and biro pen clickers."

'Travelling on public transport can be so varied in terms of interesting encounters by watching out for body language. Often it will be fascinating to subtly observe the faces of fellow passengers as various emotions flicker across their faces as they sit or stand, deep in thought. You can see the young guys of all nationalities with their restless leg syndrome twitchy legs going ten to the dozen at the same time as they feel the need to flick their hair about and pay constant homage to the mobile phone. Some people put their feet up on their seat or the opposite seat which can cause unspoken tension in others. Many sit scratching at themselves which can then make you feel itchy. The summer season brings its own amusements when insects like bees, dragonflies, moths, flies and wasps buzz in and people start waving their defensive arms and hands about like they are taking part in a Kung Fu beginners class.'

Overheard comment: A dodgy young man in his twenties trying to explain his lack of ticket to the tram conductor. It is clear he is lying. "To be honest with you chief. Yeah? I won't lie to you, honest. Yeah? As God is my witness I did have a ticket in my pocket. Yeah? I don't know where it's gone. God's truth innit, bruv?"

'Have you ever tried to descend the stairs on a double-decker bus whilst it is still moving? Not only that but add the action of gingerly trying to manoeuvre yourself downwards with one sweaty hand holding on to a bursting carrier bag of food shopping whilst your other nervous fist grips the safety rail inch by precarious inch. If you can imagine, or have experienced all that, you will understand my predicament the other week.

I only went upstairs because the downstairs section was rammed with passengers. There wasn't even room to stand. Even as I went up with my over-stuffed plastic bag of shopping I knew it wasn't the best thing to do. It was like when you watch those horror films and the stupid hero decides to nose around inside a distinctly remote, reeking of evil, pitch-black house. You can bet your boots that the crazy axe murderer is somewhere inside. "Don't do it!" you yell at the screen, but the idiot goes inside anyway. It was just the same as I grappled my way upstairs and found the only seat left. Fool that I am, I ignored the yells of common sense inside my head and carried on regardless. It's a big shame that I didn't notice that the plastic bag had a slowly expanding split on the right hand side.

As the bus was nearing my stop I got up and grabbed hold of my full to the brim bag containing fruit, cereal, pasta and rice and eggs. It had been raining, so the floor of the bus was wetter than normal and, not being very steady on my feet, I carefully and nervously edged my way towards the stairwell. The chilling horror film music, that everyone else could hear except me, jarred and swelled with jangled notes warning of dire circumstances about to occur.

I took a breath and ventured my right foot into the unknown. One wobbly step at a time, me and my bag, swayed and stumbled down the stairs. At uncertain times like this I truly hate buses. The rocking bus continued on its dark wet evening journey. When I was at my weakest position halfway down the stairs the invisible evil axe murderer suddenly struck. His concealed axe missed me yet continued its deadly downward trajectory and viciously tore into my carrier bag.

Fruit, cereal, pasta, rice and eggs tumbled from the abruptly ripped open bag and my combined vittles (there's an old fashioned word) cascaded like spilled intestines down the stairs and landed all over the lower floor of the bus. If you've ever seen and heard a grown man cry like a baby well... that was me, the other week. On the plus side I have never been upstairs with a carrier bag of shopping since. The evil axe murderer isn't going to get a second chance – no way! By the way, I've always thought that the dilapidated old house by the bus stop, looks interesting. They say it's haunted. Only a hare-brained fool would go in there. Knock knock! "Anyone at home? Hello... aaaaargh!"

Overheard comment: Woman A "I said that she said that he said that we said that they said that to her." Woman B. "I'd say nothing if I were you..."

'It seems that a certain curly haired male singer, who was very popular in the 1970s and 1980s, has latched himself very securely onto my subconscious as I travel to work this morning. It's possible he may be in my head all day. Who can predict such things? In case you are interested it is Leo Sayer, the same Leo Sayer I used to hero worship when I was in my teens and early twenties. I don't know how he got his metaphorical grappling hooks in my head so early on this day. He appears to have arrived with his very own medley of early Sayer songs on a perpetual, and not unpleasant, mental audio loop. To be clear, this is not on a mobile but just in my head.

No sooner have I sat down on the 6.30am bus out of my village to complete the first leg of a two part journey to my job in the supermarket, when the first Sayer song relays in from absolutely nowhere. I may be giving it all away to state that it is 'Givin' It All Away'. Looking back a day later, it is almost as if I remembered each snippet of a song as belonging to a particular Leo Sayer album. The next pop mix of excerpts was from the song 'Train' followed by 'Just A Boy', 'Bells of St Mary's', 'One Man Band', 'Long Tall Glasses' and 'S.O.L.O.' All of these were from his second album called, Just A Boy. Some of these songs, in parts at least, would repeat themselves as if the record had stuck and I was mentally obliged to sing out a phrase until it loosed itself from some kind of frizzy hair Top of The Pops purgatory. My inner Leo was mildly haunted by his songs all morning, afternoon and on the way home. I don't remember any other artiste even getting a look in.

I could barely stop myself twitching, singing falsetto and wildly gesticulating aka Leo Sayer as the second leg of my homeward bound journey kicked off with 'Moonlighting', 'Bedsitterland', 'The Streets of Your Town', 'Unlucky In Love' and the song of my youth and probably even adulthood, 'Only Dreaming'.

With some of the songs it was hard not start singing them out loud. I have heard people do this on public transport with or without headphones. As the bus pulled into my village that evening my Leo Sayer mental medley finished as abruptly as it had started. I was disappointed and thought "no!" 'Why Is Everybody Going Home?', 'Don't Say It's Over', surely 'The Show Must Go On'.

It didn't, but tomorrow I may accidentally conjure up my own day long Kate Bush mega mix to entertain me on my travels. It's probably a good job I never got into The Sex Pistols.

Imagine if I suddenly got carried away on the bus or tram and vehemently blurted out "I am The Anti-Christ!"

Overheard comment: "I can fit an entire double cheeseburger in my mouth and still make room for chips."

'One of my true delights is standing at a bus stop or bus shelter after a big downpour. There is usually a multitude of gigantic puddles in the surrounding streets. It is almost visually poetic. Lights are reflected in them and there are little ripples formed when people step into them or a cyclist cycles through them. Some of these deep and decidedly damp puddles like to place themselves very close to a queue of public transport users. They are the fascinating watery deposits of nature just made to be interacted with. Think David Attenborough meets Play School. Wouldn't it be fun to have a big bag full of plastic yellow ducks to play with and to drop them onto the surface of the puddles and watch them float around? Wouldn't that brighten up our commuting day? People could get to their places of work and enthral their co-workers with innocent tales of floating toy ducks on the puddles. They'd love it, I'm sure. Who wouldn't want to hear such charming stories?

Alas, I have no plastic ducks in my bag today but we do have an idiot white van driver, called Dave, who thinks it is hilarious to drive and swerve at speed directly at the mucky brown and oily puddle near me and drench me whilst I am waiting for my bus. Cheers Dave. Imagine me now, with my trousers soaking wet. I look like I have problems controlling and passing my urine and I'm sitting forlornly and exceptionally damp on the bus. Suddenly puddles are no longer the stuff of meteorological romance and plastic duck fun. They have become the base for a story of commuter revenge where I am the leader of a team of vigilante plastic ducks hell bent on tracking down idiots who are usually called Dave or Gaz, who drive white vans. Our quest may be long but me and the ducks are determined.'

Overheard comment: This lady passenger's deep and detailed conversation was with the passenger who was sitting by her. It started off with "Hello Sue..." It continued for about fifteen minutes and the woman told her friend Sue all about her life. She spoke to Sue of her family and how she was looking forward to their Christmas visit and how well her 'children' were doing in their own relationships and their working lives. Her friend Sue was gripped by this pleasantly talkative woman's stories. Eventually Sue's friend had to get off the bus and she said goodbye to Sue and how she hoped to see her again soon. The seat which Sue was sitting in was empty. It had been throughout the whole conversation.

'Today, as the Toton Lane bound tram pulled away from the QMC (Queen's Medical Centre) stop, an old chap at the front of the tram started shouting out friendly instructions to the passengers around him. The similarly aged woman with him silently looked out of the tram window at all the university buildings and parkland. I don't think she was embarrassed. She was probably just used to his unusual behaviour. I'm guessing the old fellow was a bit senile and re-living his glory days as a London bus conductor or clippie on one of the bright red London bus services. He certainly had a southern accent.

Standing up, and holding on to the rail, he shouted out several variations on "Hold Tight! Hold Tight! Elephant and Castle. Ding Ding! Any more fares please? It's ten pee to Trafalgar my darlin'. There you go my darlin'. More room on the upper deck. Move along for the lady. Ding Ding. Any more fares please? Hold Tight! Next stop Barking!" His lively and unexpected presence certainly brought a smile to the travellers on my tram today.'

Overheard comment: "And she lets her dog lick her face all the time. If you say anything she says that the dog loves her and she doesn't mind. She would if she saw how it licks its willy and then its shitty bum."

'A family I shall call, The Rainbow Family, got on my bus as I was going home today. There was Mummy Rainbow, Daddy Rainbow and their two Rainbow offspring, Bow and Rain. They were all wearing rather faded multi-coloured clothes and each one had rainbow dyed hair. In my bonkers way, I wondered to myself if it had once been that they were originally known as The Dull Family; a very average and boring family from mediocre street. Yet as fate would have it, they found themselves, one stormy day, completely by accident, all gathered together at the end of a rainbow.

At the magical point when the storm clad skies cleared, and rays of glorious July sunshine flooded the county of Nottinghamshire, The Dull Family had their Damascene moment. Bathed in a miraculous prism of light The Dull

Family were stripped of their dullness forever, yet obliged to dress like new age hippies.

I noticed that The Rainbow Family had got on the bus with a cat carrier, presumably from or to a visit to the vet. Was the cat also blessed or cursed with multi-coloured fur? We will never know until, we, one fortunate day, find ourselves at the end of a rainbow.'

Overheard comment: On the tram nearing Nottingham. One young teenage girl to another. "He's going to drive us down to London in his van. He's got some mates he's doing like a deal with. Not sure where we're stopping. His place probably. He says you can come as well. Tell your mum you're stopping at mine tonight. It'll be well good." They looked about thirteen.

'Travelling can be an adventure but also lead to disappointments. One afternoon, as my bus approached the edge of the city of Nottingham I heard someone on their mobile telling their listener where they were at that precise point in time. The speaker told their listener that they were coming up to the whale weigh station. I was intrigued because I love nature. I got off at the large building where trains come and go. It has a large glass covered concourse but imagine my mortification when there wasn't a single large marine mammal or gigantic set of scales to be seen. Obviously she was wrong. This was the railway station.'

Overheard comment: "You know last night? I was on the bus going to town and I was surrounded by Darth Vader,

Chewbaccca, Yoda, Princess Leia, Luke Skywalker and C-3PO. I thought what on Earth is going on?"

'The other day I thought I had finally conjured up my ideal morning of travel to work by bus and tram. This day seemed like one of those days that lots of commuters fantasise about – that of being the only passenger. The total joy of having no-one else around being bothersome, intrusive or downright weird. It all began by me waiting in my village for the six-thirty am bus into Nottingham. The village isn't normally that busy at stupid o'clock but this particular day it seemed even more quiet than normal. Even the birds in the trees by the church were absent in their birdy chit chat. The electronic signage, by the bus shelter, that part indicates the bus timetable and whether a bus is due, wasn't working. Nevertheless the six-thirty am number ten showed up and I got on the curiously empty bus. I was alone for the whole twenty minute journey into town. Well, of course there was the bus driver, but absolutely no passengers got on or off. Odd. Most odd.

The first time I saw anybody was at the train station Costa Coffee branch. There wasn't even a queue there like there normally is. Soon I was off on my way to the Nottingham station tram stop. On the two platforms there was just one person waiting besides me, a homeless guy. As I turned to look around he had suddenly vanished down the stairs to the train station concourse. When my tram came there was only me as a passenger for the whole eight stops to Beeston. Travelling completely alone felt like I was being transported in some sort of art film based on paintings by the American artist Edward

Hopper whose enigmatic landscapes are often peopled by a single human being.

When I got off at Beeston I headed across the empty streets to work. It was all starting to feel like I had been travelling in an alternative universe where only myself, public transport operators and coffee providers exist. The supermarket where I worked was open twenty-four hours at the time. Even when I got to work there didn't seem that many people around. Then one of the night shift workers saw me and said "You're early. Did you forget to put your clocks back an hour?" As striptease customers, often say – all was revealed.'

As Bill Bryson said of travel: "To my mind, the greatest reward and luxury of travel is to be able to experience everyday things as if for the first time, to be in a position in which nothing is so familiar it is taken for granted."

Common saying and guiding principle for this book: There's nowt as queer as folk.

Phil Lowe

Lightning Source UK Ltd.
Milton Keynes UK
UKHW022006091220
374896UK00010B/738